DIARY OF A MADMAN

OZZY
OSBOURNE

ACKNOWLEDGMENTS

With special thanks to Scott McKenzie for research, Stephanie Jones for the 'diversional reading', Diana Perkins for her practical solutions, Ian Gittins and Lorna Russell for the opportunity, Robert Smith for his swashbuckling leadership, Ozzy worldwide webmasters without whom etc etc and Nigel and Eve O'Brien, as ever, for being simply brilliant.

DIARY OF A MADMAN – OZZY OSBOURNE: THE STORIES BEHIND THE CLASSIC SONGS

Published by
Thunder's Mouth Press
An Imprint of Avalon Publishing Group Incorporated

161 William St., 16TH Floor
New York, NY 10038

Published in Great Britain by Carlton Books Limited,
20 Mortimer Street, London WIT 3JW

Library of Congress Cataloging-in-Publication Data is available

ISBN 1 56025 472 6

Project editor: Lorna Russell
Picture research: Adrian Bentley
Art Editor: Adam Wright
Design: Colin Brown,
Cover design: Alison Tutton
Production: Janette Davis
Distributed by Publishers Group West

THUNDER'S
MOUTH
PRESS

DIARY OF A MADMAN

OZZY OSBOURNE

THE STORIES BEHIND THE CLASSIC SONGS
CAROL CLERK

CONTENTS

Introduction 6

How It Happened 10

Black Sabbath 14

Paranoid 22

Master Of Reality 30

Vol 4 38

Sabbath Bloody Sabbath 44

Sabotage 52

Never Say Die 60

Blizzard Of Ozz   70

Diary Of A Madman   80

Bark At The Moon   90

**No Rest For
The Wicked**   100

No More Tears   110

Ozzmosis   120

Down To Earth   130

And so to the Present   137

Chronology   140

Discography   142

Index   144

Introduction

At the grand old age of 53, the original shock-rocker, Ozzy Osbourne, scaled new heights of superstardom, crowning his popularity – now spanning three decades – as one of the greatest characters in music and a heavy metal pioneer.

"The Osbournes", MTV's fly-on-the-wall documentary series, gripped first the United States and then Europe, with millions of viewers avidly following the hilarious exploits of a hapless Ozzy and his family at home in Los Angeles.

Generations of rock fans have adored the larger-than-life persona of the former Black Sabbath frontman, whose behaviour has been idiotic as often as his proclamations have been rudely insightful. Always compelling and endlessly funny, Ozzy has at the same time managed to affront the moral majority during a lifetime of tabloid headlines. Religious and civic leaders – and outraged parents – have risen against him at every twist and turn of his colourful career.

He was branded a devil-worshipper from the earliest days, while also being threatened by Satanists. He was stalked by covens, blamed for stabbings and sued for "encouraging" suicides. He bit the heads off a bat and a dove, both alive at the time. He threw raw meat at his audiences and "hung" a dwarf onstage. He pissed on the revered Alamo in Texas. He drank as much as possible, took excessive quantities of drugs, and during one terrible altercation, tried to kill his wife and manager, Sharon.

Ozzy Osbourne has risen above these and other notorious escapades by virtue of an irrepressible personality – and serious musical credentials. Widely credited with inventing heavy metal music, Ozzy and Black Sabbath took the early 1970s by storm with a particular brand of dark, weighty, riff-driven rock that would become a blueprint for countless imitators. Yet Ozzy never rested on his laurels, perpetually diversifying; a tender ballad was as much in character as a turbo-charged tirade against society.

The Osbournes: Ozzy is cheered on by Sharon, Kelly and Jack as he receives his star on the Hollywood Walk Of Fame

Eager to spot new talent but avoid the old-boy network, he actively sought out and recruited young musicians like Randy Rhoads and Zakk Wylde, who would subsequently become heroes in their own right.

Ozzy's personal circumstances are often reflected in the music he made as he lurched in and out of rehab (eventually giving up alcohol and substance abuse), confronted deranged followers and protesters, fought contractual battles in court, defended himself against allegations that his music was a dangerous influence on youngsters, and saw many of his friends and colleagues succumb to illness or die from the lifestyle that he himself once heartily embraced.

Ozzy – an inveterate and preposterous rocker worthy

Ozzy: a fringe entertainer

of *Spinal Tap* – was never the "dark lord" people claimed. Much of this reputation came about by accident and was only then built into the personality of the onstage showman. That he now festoons his mansion with crucifixes, skulls, "dead things", guns and bayonets is more than anything a tribute to the cartoon fantasy that the public encouraged, expected, received and celebrated. It was a reciprocal, tongue-in-cheek, not blood-on-parchment, agreement, although there were deluded souls who desperately wanted to believe in the singer's occult superiority.

In reality, Ozzy's repertoire reveals something of a humanitarian. He has sung about everything from the LA riots to the nuclear arms race, the escalating problems of "crack babies" and paedophilia, the rise of pornography, the hypocrisy of religion and a Lennon-esque ability to imagine all the people living life in peace.

Sentimental about his departure from Black Sabbath, his family and the deaths of the Small Faces' Steve Marriott and AC/DC's Bon Scott, he also talks, through his records, about sex, drugs and rock'n'roll, relationships and the journey of the spirit after death.

After some time on rock's back burner, Ozzy re-emerged as a major player in 1996 when he established his popular Ozzfest roadshows, typically eager to share his stages with the most promising and exciting young metal talents of the day.

Nothing, however, could have prepared him for the monumental success awaiting him with "The Osbournes", a human soap opera which finds a sober but befuddled Ozzy shambling around his massive home trying unsuccessfully to work the television, wondering what the fuck that noise could be (a ringing telephone), wringing his hands over the untrained toilet habits of his numerous dogs and cats, and reeling with confusion and exasperation as he tries to keep up with the doings of his wife and children.

Usually described as a "dysfunctional family", the Osbournes are unconventional, unpredictable and in their own inimitable way, both tolerant and loving: a Simpsons for the twenty-first century.

This book, however, looks back on the life and times of Ozzy Osbourne through his recorded achievements, both as a dramatic interpreter of songs in Black Sabbath and as a writer and co-writer for his own groups throughout the Eighties and Nineties. It remembers the changing line-ups of his bands, brings anecdotes from the studios, revisits the lyrics, the artwork and the ongoing musical changes, and investigates the surrounding controversies.

This is Ozzy Osbourne – not through a lens, but through the timeless medium of his material.

How it Happened

Black Sabbath came together in Birmingham, England, at the tail end of the Sixties. Ozzy Osbourne, Tony Iommi, Geezer Butler and Bill Ward had grown up in Aston, a Birmingham suburb proud of its own identity and its independence from the city. Thrashed by German bombs during World War II, it was a place where people clocked into jobs for life in the local factories, spent their evenings playing darts and getting drunk in the pubs, and living in cramped, old houses that, in true British working-class tradition, they kept scrupulously clean and bright.

A genuine sense of community pervaded the area, despite the real poverty, but there existed, at the same time, a violent street culture. The increasing numbers of teenagers forming bands not only escaped the grim realities of everyday life but also managed to sidestep the invitations of the local gangs.

As pop's golden decade drew to a close, as the hippies sang optimistically of love and peace, many of the up-and-coming players were attracted to the grittier, less commercial, but more musicianly sound of the white, urban blues. A burgeoning scene in the clubs and drinking dens of London and other British cities, including Birmingham, it would produce some of the world's most revered rock stars.

Tony Iommi (born Anthony Frank Iommi on February 19, 1948) and Bill Ward (born William Thomas Ward on May 5, 1948) cut their teeth playing guitar and drums in a straight blues band first called The Rest and then Mythology. They moved to Carlisle, a base for touring the north of England, and built a solid following before the group split up and the pair returned to Aston.

John Michael Osbourne (born December 3, 1948), was at that time calling himself Ozzy Zig and looking for musical opportunities, having decided to abandon a spectacularly unsuccessful career as a thief and burglar. He has since declared that, "Music saved me from becoming a hardened criminal."

Ozzy suffered more than his share of hardship as a child. His father, Jack, a steel worker, and his mother, Lillian, a factory worker in the Lucas car assembly shop, struggled to feed and clothe their growing family of six children – three boys and three girls.

Dyslexic and suffering from Attention Deficit Disorder, Ozzy was simply dismissed as a "thick" pupil at school, and he achieved little academically. But he acquired a taste for the stage, taking part in operetta productions, and he learned the value of entertainment, clowning around to amuse and befriend the school bullies rather than invite their hostilities.

However, there was no love lost between Ozzy and a fellow-pupil by the name of Tony Iommi.

"I used to hate the sight of Ozzy," Iommi later admitted. "I couldn't stand him, and I used to beat him up whenever I saw him. We just didn't get on at school. He was a little punk."

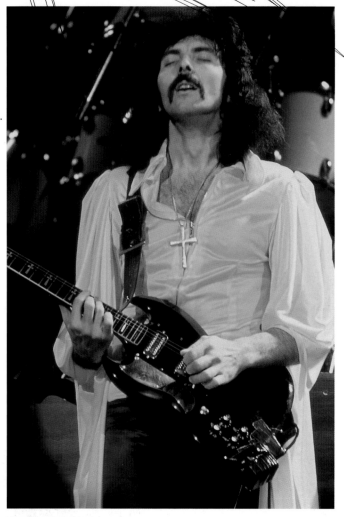

Tony Iommi: an innovator

Leaving school early to start earning, the "little punk" took on a succession of jobs, working for a plumber, a toolmaker and, for little more than a week, a mortuary. He was also a mechanic, he painted houses and he tuned car horns in the Lucas factory, later remarking, "I liked heavy metal better because it was louder."

Famously, he spent a couple of years in a Digbeth abattoir, recently recalling: "There was a giant mountain of sheep's stomachs and my job was to get this knife and cut them up and empty the puke out of the stomachs. I was so tired of throwing up, my eyes were bulging out of my head from straining. Everyone who eats meat should walk through an abattoir. You will not take four steps without puking your guts out. I guarantee."

But it was "much better" than tuning car horns.

Better still was the lure of easy money from crime. Ozzy started out by breaking into a local clothes shop. He did it again and was caught.

He said later, "I was the Norman Wisdom of burgling. I did everything wrong, like wearing gloves with the fingers out."

Legend has it that on one occasion, he fell off a wall and was flattened by a stolen TV set he'd been carrying.

Finally, Ozzy broke into a boarding house with a workmate, only to be apprehended and beaten senseless by the owner and then charged with burglary, larceny, assault and possession of dope. Unable to pay the fine, he served two months in Winson Green prison in 1965, emerging with tattoos and a determination to stay out of jail.

After being rejected by the Army – perhaps the top brass weren't impressed by the pyjama top he was wearing – Ozzy threw himself into music, inspired by Fifties' American rock'n'roll, The Beatles and an ambition to "have fun, fuck chicks and do drugs".

He'd actually made his debut at the age of 14 in an outfit called The Black Panthers. Now, he deputized for the singer of a band called Music Machine, and he joined Approach, a group he didn't actually like and quickly left.

But he had a lucky break when he met rookie rhythm guitarist Geezer Butler (born Terence Michael Butler on July 17, 1949) and formed the short-lived Rare Breed. They came together when the singer placed an advertisement in a local music shop: "Ozzy Zig, vocalist, requires band", using as bait the fact that he had his own PA (bought by his father).

Tony Iommi, responding to the appeal with Bill Ward, was horrified to discover not only that this was the Ozzy Osbourne of his schooldays but also that the singer had short hair.

Nevertheless, after some to-ing and fro-ing, Ozzy started growing his locks and joined Geezer, Tony and Bill in a jazzy blues band with extraneous members, including a slide guitarist and a saxophonist, who were soon dropped.

Regrouping, with Geezer switching from rhythm guitar to bass, the four-piece swiftly ditched their improbable name, The Polka Tulk Blues Band, then shortened to Polka Tulk, to become Earth. (Interestingly, a drone-rock band from the Seattle grunge scene years later would call themselves Earth in tribute to their heroes, with founding guitarist Dylan Carlson rising to infamy after buying the shotgun that Nirvana's Kurt Cobain used to commit suicide in 1994.)

During 1969, Ozzy took his first steps into serious showmanship, on one occasion painting his face and feet purple, to the reported apathy of Earth's German audience.

The band acquired a manager, jazz trumpeter Jim Simpson, who booked them into a local venue called Henry's – where a hopeful Led Zeppelin had also been spreading their wings.

"We just wanted to be heavier than everyone else."

It was at Henry's that Earth realized they would have to change their name; the audience was expecting another group of the same name, and were far from thrilled with the heavy blues-rock which bombarded them.

Earth became Black Sabbath – a choice which has since been explained in several different ways. Some say it reflected Geezer Butler's interest in the black arts and authors such as Dennis Wheatley. Others contend that it was simply taken from the name of the track "Black Sabbath", which already existed. According to Ozzy, the name came from a chance comment by Tony Iommi, who'd seen the ancient Boris Karloff movie *Black Sabbath* billed at the cinema near the rehearsal studio they were working in.

Noting that people were happy to shell out money to be scared, Iommi suggested that the band should play frightening music. "When he came up with that 'Black Sabbath' riff," said Ozzy, "that was the scariest riff I've ever heard in my life." He has also insisted: "I liked the name Black Sabbath because of the succession of vowel sounds."

The band were influenced by the likes of Hendrix, Cream and Ten Years After, whose dazzling guitarist Alvin Lee lent a helping hand by arranging for them to play at the legendary Marquee club in London – their first step up the ladder.

Geezer Butler told writer John Stix: "That started the ball rolling for us. We were up against bands that were just starting, like Ten Years After, Jethro Tull and Zeppelin. We knew we had to be as good as them to make a go of it. We knew we had to practise every day… also, you had to be totally different from anybody else to get recognized, whereas now you've got a lot of bands doing heavy metal and that's it."

Still, Black Sabbath had little idea of their massive potential, seeing themselves simply as "a really heavy 12-bar blues band". What swung it was this: "We just wanted to be heavier than everybody else."

Black Sabbath

"My parents had the first Black Sabbath album in their collection. I remember when I first put it on, it scared me a little bit. It was dark, in its sound and in what was being said. I was immediately attracted to it. I guess that was the part of me that really wanted to get it, because it felt like that had been suppressed for so many years. It kinda just opened me up. I've said this before: Black Sabbath was my introduction into heavy metal."

MARILYN MANSON

The album *Black Sabbath* was recorded (on eight tracks) and mixed in two days for a mere few hundred pounds while the band were on the hop between England and a residency in Switzerland. Working with producer Rodger Bain, they played more or less live, an approach that empowered the material with the band's own thunderous sense of purpose.

Released by Vertigo on Friday the 13th, February 1970, the album received mixed reviews from the music press but nevertheless climbed to number eight in the UK charts. It was to be 42 weeks before it dropped out of the listings.

Issued five months later in America by Warners, it made a decent showing at number 23.

Nothing so unrelentingly heavy, so bleak, so loud, had been heard before in polite rock society. Butler and Ward created a ponderous and often unconventional bedrock for Iommi's distorted guitar, his gloomy riffs and power chords. Generations of bands have since aimed to recreate Iommi's deafening, guitar overdrive.

Ozzy recently remarked: "Right up to this day, Tony Iommi is one of the innovators of heavy metal guitar playing. This is no small thing considering he chopped off the ends of his middle and ring fingers on a machine."

Creating an unholy alliance with Iommi's grungy guitar strokes came Ozzy's unsophisticated caterwauling – a vocal technique which he claims to have copied from his father's pissed-up singalongs at home in Aston, Birmingham.

Jack Osbourne was clearly a man of much influence. Ozzy recalled: "My old man used to say, 'You've got to give people a tune so they've got something to sing after they've had a few pints of Newcastle Brown and it's cold by the bus stop.' Sabbath might be heavy, but there's always the melody in there that makes us what we are."

It was Jack, too, who made aluminium crosses at work for the four-piece – Ozzy later had his copied in gold – and these contributed to the devilish imagery surrounding the rising Black Sabbath.

The addition of an inverted cross to the album's artwork, allegedly without the band's prior agreement, strengthened their perceived connections with the occult. This had been the idea of some bright spark at Vertigo records, acting on the imagery suggested by both the music and the lyrics.

Wordsmith Geezer Butler was indeed preoccupied by the shadowy side of life. In his attempts at poetry, he dwelled in a depressing, medieval, fantasy world where anger, fear and menace loomed large, death walked behind you and in front of you, and spiritual or Satanic encounters could reasonably be expected, if not encouraged. Black Sabbath's debut album was accordingly condemned as "evil" and "blasphemous" by parents, Christians and other fearful parties, particularly in America.

This would cause great problems for the group in the months and years ahead. But the campaigners' outrage was tumultuously answered by a teenage audience thrilled to find a band who would rock their speakers, shock their elders and open up a forbidden new playground for the imagination.

"When we came out of *The Exorcist*, we had to stay in one room together – that's how black magic *we* were," said Ozzy, a most unlikely warlock, even in those days. He explained: "Black Sabbath was never really a Satanic band, although we did touch on topics like Satanism and devil worship in certain songs. It was just a different angle."

Admitting freely that he has always seen his character as a "theatrical role", he is also quoted as saying: "Sabbath was a reaction against all these stupid bands around at the time going on about young love and boy meets girl. It seemed to us this was more like real life… I can honestly tell you, there was no inner

Geezer Butler: Lord of the night

secret, no fuckin' black magic. It was just four guys doing whatever they could…"

More recently, he commented: "You gotta think of the time. It was all this fucking bells and hippies and smoking dope and free-love shit, and we just thought, 'It ain't like that, really.' When you're living in Birmingham and it's fucking raining every day and you've got no money in your pocket and you get this bullshit – that just wasn't right to us.

"I lived in Aston and my dad was fucking dying of industrial pollution. What the fuck did I care about fucking flowers and that hippie shit?… The only flower you saw in Aston was on a fucking gravestone."

And just in case there was any lingering confusion: "When we did the first album, it wasn't like we sat around a fucking campfire burning virgins at the stake or anything… We didn't slaughter a first-born son on the tape machine. We just got as pissed as farts."

Black Sabbath

The doom-laden title track of the band's first album has become one of the great rock classics of all time. From beginning to end, from the eerie, opening sounds of a rainstorm and a church bell through the monstrous riffs and sinister melodies that lead to a climactic guitar solo, this is archetypal Sabbath.

The genuinely disturbing music is matched by a set of lyrics about a smirking Satan who is chasing his "chosen one" – the song's narrator – as the flames of hell burn ever higher and the victim flees, with Ozzy wailing, "Oh, no!" and pleading, "Please God, help me!"

It's a scenario which should logically have been interpreted as a fantasy that, if anything, clearly warned against any forays into the black arts, but this was overlooked by listeners who preferred to link the track and the very mention of the word Satan to the overwhelming body of evidence – the aluminium crosses, the album sleeve, the musical force – that had

already placed Ozzy, Iommi, Butler and Ward on the dark side of the spiritual fence.

The track pre-dated the band's change of name to Black Sabbath, erupting spontaneously in a humble four-track studio in London's Tottenham Court Road, where they were recording demos. Ozzy recalled a simple sequence of events: "We started writing heavy riffs, wrote the song 'Black Sabbath' and then we changed our name."

"'Black Sabbath' was written on bass," Geezer Butler recalled in *Bass Frontiers* magazine. "I just went into the studio and went, 'Bah, bah, bah,' and everybody joined in and we just did it. However long the song is was how long it took us to write it. Like 'N.I.B.' just started with me doing the bass riff and everybody joined in. In those days, we didn't have tape recorders or anything, and nobody would write stuff at home and bring it to the studio. We just used to jam for two or three hours and see what came out."

Ozzy would spontaneously weigh in with melody lines and the odd lyric and Iommi, well, he was the man who most often sparked the songs, just messing around on the guitar. He was, according to Ozzy, "the master of fucking riffs".

Even more generously, the singer adds: "We never realized at the time how fucking clever he was." With each song worked out on the spot, Geezer Butler would later add vocals.

While Geezer sees "Black Sabbath" as a bass-driven creation, Iommi vividly remembers it springing to life from a guitar riff that simply came to him, and Ward – who drummed with his body, heart, soul and massive cymbals – cites the track as a particularly good example of his tom-tom work and swing rhythms.

But every member of the band agrees that "Black Sabbath" – like the other album tracks – happened almost by itself; they never had to wait for the elusive muse. Bill Ward, for one, believes they were being guided…

"When we did the first album, it wasn't like we sat around a fucking campfire burning virgins at the stake or anything… We didn't slaughter a first-born son on the tape machine. We just got as pissed as farts."

"... just four guys doing whatever they could."

The Wizard

Tony Iommi enjoyed Geezer's interest in the supernatural: he was delighted that it separated the group from their contemporaries, and it particularly suited his enormous, gates-of-hell guitar riffing.

But the abrasive motif he contributed to "The Wizard" was perhaps out of step with the lyrics, which are rightly regarded as an embarrassment – they are too cheery, too primary school.

Dressed with harmonica, the song talks of evil powers and demons – all well and good except that these forces from the underworld come over all worried and "magically disappear" when the wizard strolls through the neighbourhood wearing fancy clothes, ringing a bell and casting a benevolent spell or two. The possibility exists that the wizard might be intended as a characterization of God and the song as a cynical comment on worshippers' blind faith, although this is not specified in the lyric.

Whatever, the respectable citizens in the song are relieved to be rid of the fiendish dangers – they all "give a happy sigh", which isn't exactly what you might expect from Black Sabbath, two tracks into their controversial first album.

Ozzy, however, still defends the imagery: "If a wizard walked up to you, you'd definitely go, 'Fuck me, there's a wizard!'" The track would later turn up as the B-side for the band's future hit single, "Paranoid".

N.I.B.

The meaning of the title has long been debated, with many fans believing that it stands for "Nativity In Black". But according to Ozzy, it represents something much less mysterious.

He explained: "We were all stoned in Hamburg and Bill used to have this really long, pointy beard and I said, 'Hey Bill, you look like a pen nib.' So when Geezer said, 'What are we going to call this song?' I said, 'Oh, call it N.I.B.'"

The title, therefore, is completely unconnected to the track, which is lyrically fanciful, imagining a scenario in which the Beast himself has fallen in love – "Look into

my eyes, you'll see who I am/My name is Lucifer, please take my hand."

"There's only two songs that even mention Satan or Lucifer on the first album," said Geezer Butler in a 1997 interview. "The song 'Black Sabbath'… and 'N.I.B.' is a tongue-in-cheek thing about how Lucifer would feel about everything if he fell in love with someone, which I thought was a reasonably humorous thing to write about.

"But, of course, people in America just picked up on the words Satan and Lucifer, didn't listen to any of the other lyrics and condemned us. Which is sad, because some of my other Black Sabbath lyrics – 'After Forever' (from 1971's *Master Of Reality*) as an example – are as religious as anything you'll ever read."

Returning to the topic of black magic, Ozzy sighed: "No matter how much you'd tell these people it's not for real, they'd go, 'Oh yeah, but we know,' and wink. Even

N.I.B.' on our first album was a humorous song about the Devil falling in love, and I thought it was hysterical. But nobody got the point…"

EVIL WOMAN (DON'T PLAY YOUR GAMES WITH ME)

Black Sabbath's first single, backed with "Wicked World", was released twice within three months – first by Fontana in January 1970 and again in March when the group moved to the Vertigo label.

"Evil Woman", slightly more commercial than the rest of the album tracks, was a cover of a song by a Minnesota band called Crow and another of the cuts emerging from the Regent Sound sessions in Tottenham Court Road.

The single flopped both times, but Ozzy was unconcerned. It was enough for him that he had made a

Black Sabbath – straight outta Aston

record to take home and show his mother. It didn't occur to him, or to his fellow bandmates, that the original material they were irrepressibly coming up with would become their passport to untold wealth and infamy.

But they did realize that they had hit on something different and extremely powerful, almost without trying. Bill Ward is reluctant to take any of the credit for this. In an extraordinary interview with author Steven Rosen, he talked of the spooky coincidences that occurred during the band's early years, with all four members, on one occasion, reporting the same dream. He also claimed there was a fifth, invisible member of Black Sabbath.

"The fifth member of Black Sabbath was whatever the phenomenon was," he told Rosen in all seriousness. "A lot of the times we didn't write the fucking songs at all. We showed up and something else wrote them for us. We were conduits."

Ward revealed that Ozzy's father, Jack, was aware of some strangeness around the band, recognizing that, "there was something going on here that possibly he couldn't understand, but he knew it was real…" Jack also knew that, "there'd been some kind of phenomenon going on here that nobody was quite sure of".

Ozzy is less dramatic about his father's reactions to Black Sabbath, recently saying: "I remember when the first album came out I thought, 'Great, I can show my dad.' We put it on the old radiogram and I remember him looking at Mum with this really confused look on his face and turning to me and saying, 'Son, are you sure you're just drinking the occasional beer?'"

Other tracks on the album are "Behind The Wall Of Sleep" ("I always thought that your dreams were telling you what death was going to be like, after a particularly weird dream I had," said Geezer) and the four-line poem that is "Sleeping Village", an unsettling, acoustic snippet segueing into the blues-influenced "Warning", which laments a lost love and includes a long guitar solo. It was longer still, around 18 minutes, before being cut in the mix, much to Iommi's disappointment.

The extended US tracklisting features: "Black Sabbath", "The Wizard", "Wasp", "Behind The Wall Of Sleep", "Basically", "N.I.B.", "Wicked World", "A Bit Of Finger", "Sleeping Village" and "Warning".

The amazing, vanishing Bill Ward and his enormous drumkit

Paranoid

"Back in the day, my cousin had a Sabbath
album opened up and I was like, 'Damn, this guy's voice
is awesome.' I saw that video, "Paranoid" and Ozzy's hair was
all in his face, and he was just singing. I mean, you
can't help but like Ozzy Osbourne: his voice, his melody,
his music, his everything is great."

FRED DURST, LIMP BIZKIT

With the *Paranoid* album, Black Sabbath truly arrived. Honouring and exceeding all the promises of their debut, this was a triumph, a headbanger's paradise, a true metal classic.

Black Sabbath had been the sound of a band working their way, instinctively, towards something massive. *Paranoid* was it.

Like their Brummie contemporaries Led Zeppelin – who'd been first to release an album – Sabbath transformed the blues of their early experience into a raw, original and devastating music that would change the rock landscape forever.

Unlike Zeppelin, Black Sabbath counted only one gifted musician in the band. That was Tony Iommi. Ozzy, Geezer and Bill were impulsive and emotional rather than skilful, which probably accounts for the impassioned, sledgehammer energy with which they set about their business. Also unlike Zeppelin, Sabbath steered clear of songs about sex. Geezer, as a lyricist, had more to worry about than the simple pleasures of the flesh. This was fortunate. Ozzy may have been a well-loved frontman, but he was never going to compete with the golden Robert Plant as a chest-baring love god. Again unlike Zeppelin, Black Sabbath were indifferent to subtlety, to adventurous arrangement. Determinedly primitive, they wanted only to bludgeon their songs and their listeners into glorious submission.

"The reason we appeal to so many people so instantly is because our sound is good and basic," said Ozzy at the time. "It doesn't take a lot of understanding. The impact is right there."

That impact, many believe, gave birth to heavy metal – but Ozzy's not that proud. Recently, he fumed: "All that stuff about heavy metal and hard rock – I don't subscribe to any of that. It's all just music. I mean, the heavy metal from the Seventies sounds nothing like the

Led Zeppelin: released their first album before Black Sabbath

stuff from the Eighties, and that sounds nothing like the stuff from the Nineties. Who's to say what is and isn't a certain type of music?

"I've always hated the term heavy metal. We didn't start Black Sabbath and say, 'Right, we're gonna play metal.' We just played scary music, and at some bright spot we called it heavy metal, and it went on from there."

Geezer Butler reasoned: "When you write your first album, you're influenced by all the stuff that's going on around you, and I think each one of us brought our own particular styles into the music that we did. So in the beginning, all the different influences you've had up until then come together on one album, and from there it gells into this one sound rather than lots of different things.

"When you realize you've got your own sound, then you can just pick up on that and keep it going in one direction. I thought it happened on the *Paranoid* album. On the first one, we didn't really know what we were doing."

Among the other innovations attributed to Black Sabbath is the great institution of headbanging. Bill

Ward told Steven Rosen about the changing appearances and rituals of the Sabbath audiences, remembering: "Headbanging started in the clubs, through Ozzy… We wouldn't let anybody sit down. That was a no-no. Suddenly, everybody was up in the clubs and we were rocking."

When the *Paranoid* album was unleashed in September 1970, Black Sabbath raised the stakes. The album was a UK Number One hit, residing in the charts for 27 weeks. It almost crashed into the American Top 10 as well, peaking at number 12, following the album's release in the US in February 1971. As a result, Black Sabbath would start a long relationship with the American highway.

Paranoid was obviously less blues influenced and had less of a jam-session sound than the first album; it sounded rockier, more ominous. And it was the first big hitter in a career that would influence generations of every different type of metal band, as well as goths, punks, post-punks, grunge rockers, rock'n'rollers, hardcore outfits and even funk-rock acts like the Red

Hot Chili Peppers.

At the same time, Sabbath were so utterly serious about their music and their often preposterous lyrics that, to some observers, they were merely hilarious. Elements of Sabbath are identifiable in the great spoof metal movie, *This is Spinal Tap*, not least in the character of Derek Smalls whose long, dark hair and drooping moustache are pure Geezer Butler.

Like its predecessor, *Paranoid* was written by the group's invisible fifth member, according to Bill Ward. More factual historians state that the songs came together quickly, often on the road, and were recorded on 24 tracks, to Iommi's great excitement, at Regent Sound and Island Studios in a matter of days.

WAR PIGS

"War Pigs" was the proposed album title as well as a phenomenal opening track. Described in *Guitar World* as "the greatest HM song ever", it begins with the immortal couplet: "Generals gathered in their

masses/Just like witches at black masses."

The song started life as "Walpurgis" or, as Geezer puts it, "Satan's Christmas thing". But because of the furore surrounding Black Sabbath and their alleged involvement in black magic, they decided to re-write the lyrics, and "War Pigs" became a protest song, condemning the war in Vietnam and the hypocrisies of the politicians and the propagandists who sent young men off to die in the jungles.

In typical Sabbath style, the "war pigs" reap what they've sown when Judgement Day finds them crawling on their knees, begging forgiveness, while "Satan, laughing, spreads his wings". Legend has it that Sabbath heard horror stories about the war from soldiers they were entertaining at an American Air Force base, but Ozzy, while conceding that the song is about Vietnam, contends: "We knew nothing about Vietman. It's just an anti-war song."

The record company refused to accept *War Pigs* as the album title due to American sensitivities over Vietnam, and settled on *Paranoid* instead.

However, there was no time to change the sleeve artwork, so *Paranoid* is rather ineffectually illustrated by a man running out of a forest with a helmet, sword and shield.

"War Pigs" was a great favourite of the late Zeppelin drummer, John Bonham, Ward's drinking buddy. Ward told Steven Rosen: "John was a big fan of Black Sabbath… he would play on my kit and he would make the kit sing…

"He liked what I did with the hi-hat. But he was always jiving me about how I had too many drums and said, 'These (Zeppelin) bastards won't let me have any drums.'"

"Considering we recorded it in three-and-a-half minutes, it's not bad."

Bonham particularly liked "Supernaut" and "Cornucopia", both from the *Vol. 4* album.

PARANOID

Estimates range between five and 30 minutes. That's how long it took for Black Sabbath (or Ward's handy fifth member) to write and arrange the band's most famous anthem. It was a last-minute effort, a quick space-filler at the end of the main recording sessions, and it was perfect.

Ozzy said: "I remember Rodger Bain (the producer) saying: 'We need three or four minutes to finish the album.' So Tony came up with the riff, I came up with the melody, Geezer wrote the lyrics and it was done within 10 minutes. Geezer didn't even know what the word 'paranoid' meant, but people were always calling him that, so he made it the title of the song."

Ozzy also suggested that, "The best songs always happen that way. You can sit down and plan and fucking work it out, but it's those quickies that turn out the best." And he added: "Considering we recorded it in three-and-a-half minutes, it's not bad."

Released as a single in August 1970, "Paranoid" reached number four in the UK and stayed in the chart for 18 weeks. In the US, three months later, it registered at number 61.

While *Paranoid* is still the people's favourite Sabbath album, "Paranoid" the single remains highly rated in polls of greatest-ever rock tracks, and in 1995, it won

Tony Iommi a *Kerrang!* award for "Best Guitar Riff Ever".

But its success 25 years earlier came as a mixed blessing, attracting a new, young and very excitable crowd to Sabbath gigs. Ozzy said of one gig at Portsmouth: "There were kids rushing down the front and girls screaming and grabbing us. We couldn't believe it…

"We don't need fans like those. We'll just have to

grin and bear them and they'll go away. We're not changing our stage act to please the kids who just bought the single."

Problems were also reported in Newcastle, where the crowd surged uncontrollably on to the stage, destroying a PA speaker and a bass drum microphone and thieving Ward's drumsticks and cymbals.

Ozzy said at the time: "If it means us having to give up putting out singles, then we will. We want people to listen to us, not try to touch us. I was really terrified, shocked out of my mind."

IRON MAN

Another Sabbath monster, the melancholic "Iron Man", with its massive riff, also became an immediate crowd favourite. "I am Iron Man!" warns Ozzy on the record, acting out his dramatic role to the full.

It was Ozzy who suggested the title to an inspired

Geezer Butler. Geezer, who was responsible for almost all of the band's lyrics, said: "Ozzy might come up with a line at the time when we were writing the stuff. He was humming along and said, 'Iron Man'."

Geezer continued: "I wrote it about this guy who's blasted off into space and sees the future of the world, which isn't very good. Then he goes through a magnetic storm on the way back and is turned into iron.

"He's trying to warn everyone about the future, but he can't speak, so everyone is taking the mickey out of him all the time, and he just doesn't care in the end."

"He goes a bit barmy and decides to get his revenge by killing people," added Ozzy. "He tries to do good, but in the end, it turns into bad."

Released in the US in January 1972, "Iron Man" reached Number 52, making it the group's highest-charting single in America.

Hand of Doom

Unusually for Black Sabbath, the lyrics wagged a finger at themselves.

There had been a tradition of alcohol and drugs, mainly dope, around the band from their earliest days. And in years to come, with money no object, they would be unrivalled in their capacity to devour illicit substances, with stories abounding of days-long marathons and supplies of cocaine being delivered to the door in cereal cartons.

Bill Ward has admitted that his most enduring memory of the period leading up to the *Paranoid* album is of taking drugs, specifically hash. He was also a fearless drinker, regularly out on the rampage with a voracious John Bonham.

Tony Iommi has also recalled the excessive drinking during this time, which went on for years to come. His

John Bonham: regularly out on the rampage with Bill Ward

bandmates, he said, were often so drunk they left him on his own, effectivelyhanding him the responsibility of delivering an entire album's worth of new ideas. He didn't disappoint – but freely admits he was no saint himself.

Iommi would later suffer from memory loss relating to his own recreational pursuits. He recalled that pills, all sorts of pills, came into the picture around the time of *Paranoid*. And strong, new alliances with acid and cocaine were just around the corner.

However, the warnings dished out sternly in "Hand Of Doom" speak of heavier stuff altogether. Graphically depicting a mainlining junkie, the lyrics urge: "Push the needle in/Face death's sickly grin" before climaxing, vividly, with an overdose.

While the song ostensibly centres on an army veteran trying to blot out the horrors of Vietnam, it's widely believed that the drugs references were to some extent personal, confessional, even accusatory.

The tragedy unfolds as suspense, drama and tempos build within a harrowing soundtrack – one credited with spawning the sub-genre of doom metal, which depends on "heaviness, darkness, sadness, depression and melancholy".

Undeniably, "Hand Of Doom" is a textbook mixture of these requirements, along with other tracks from the band's repertoire. Sabbath were simply the first of the forefathers.

Fairies Wear Boots

Skinhead thugs were attracting a lot of critcism in the UK at this time, particularly from Black Sabbath who had fallen victim to a gang attack.

This reportedly happened on the night of the Newcastle stage invasion, with the band being set upon as they walked through the streets after the show. Tony Iommi sustained painful arm injuries in the fracas, and the band were forced to call off their next gig in the touring schedule.

In the pre-politically correct world of the time, Sabbath retaliated by abusing the boot-boys who had beaten them up in the way which would most insult them – as "fairies".

Varying the pace and style before launching into a solid and satisfyingly raucous charge, Ozzy relishes a lyric which sneers: "Fairy boots were dancin' with a dwarf/All right now!"

The song is eager to incorporate another hint at drugs consumption with descriptions of a visit to the doctor: "He said, 'Son, son, you've gone too far/Cause smokin' and trippin' is all that you do.'"

Other tracks on the album are the almost balladic "Planet Caravan", which is slow, evocative, spacey and a little unnerving, Ozzy's vocals treated with some primitive, electronic device; the thuddingly morbid "Electric Funeral"; and the guitar and drum showcase of "Rat Salad".

MASTER OF REALITY

"The first stuff that had
a real impact on me was
Master Of Reality.
In my head, that was the way music
should sound."
BILLY CORGAN,
THE SMASHING PUMPKINS

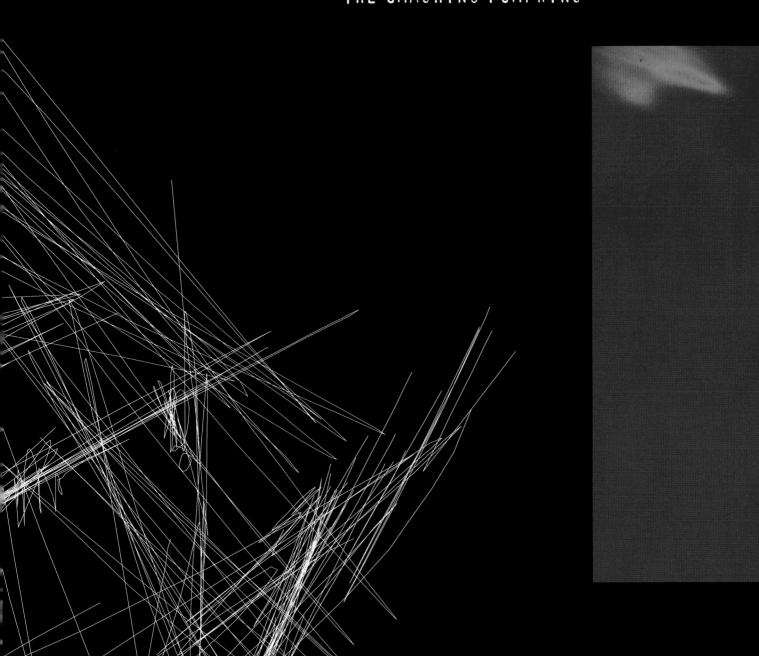

It's been described as the heaviest album ever. If Sabbath had felt under pressure to repeat the stellar success of *Paranoid*, they responded proudly with *Master Of Reality*, a confident resumption of their trademark, brutal minimalism and a testament to Tony Iommi's mastery of the rock guitar.

Looking back on it only a couple of years ago, Ozzy remarked: "I think *Master Of Reality* was a great album. Nobody would dare to do what we were doing and get away with it. We defied all fucking realms of commerciality and got accepted." He once memorably proposed that early Sabbath songs "sound as if they're covered in mud from a Colombian volcano".

Recording at London's Olympic Studios and occasionally taking advantage of the opportunities for effects and overdubs, they retained their monstrous clump but began to branch out lyrically.

Their most sensational departure was with "After Forever", in which Geezer Butler's verses campaigned for God with all the evangelism of a born-again Christian. It sounded strange indeed, from the mouth of Ozzy Osbourne! The song was, perhaps, an attempt to break free from the black magic mantle that was firmly wrapped around Sabbath, especially in America.

Playing there to promote *Paranoid* and *Master Of Reality*, the band revelled in the pleasures of sex, drugs and rock'n'roll – Ozzy's first experience of cocaine was on their debut American tour, playing with Mountain – and they were at the centre of some quite astonishing events. They received death threats, were ordered to defend their music to mayors and police departments nervous about letting the gigs go ahead, had shows called off, were cheered in LA by members of Charles Manson's "family", and in San Francisco, had a procession held in their honour by Anton LaVey, High Priest of the Church of Satan and author of the *Satanic Bible*. Black Sabbath, the "devil's disciples" feared by all America, had never even heard of LaVey. "We just thought, 'What the fuck?'" said Ozzy.

Back in these early days, there was an endearing naivety about Ozzy in particular, who seemed genuinely bewildered at the extreme reactions that Sabbath provoked. "I remember when we started getting invites to black masses," he said. "We all looked at each other and said, 'Is this for real or what?'"

Sabbath probably just thought "What the fuck?" in Memphis too, where they found their dressing room walls smeared with crosses of blood, and where one deranged character sprang onto the stage brandishing a sacrificial knife.

Later, a crowd of people – said to be the local coven – assembled outside their hotel, where Geezer Butler reputedly tried to frighten them off by pretending to put a hex on them.

Ozzy recalled: "I went to my hotel room. There were about 15 freaks outside my door with black-painted faces and robes and daggers and candles. I slammed the door and phoned the roadie. I said, 'There are a load of cuckoo brains out there.'

"The roadie got them all round with their candles, said, 'Happy birthday', blew the candles out and told them to clear off. I used to get people like that sleeping in corridors outside my room wherever we went. They got into the literal side of Black Sabbath, searching out meanings."

Geezer Butler said: "The whole Satanism thing was a big surprise for us when we came to America. The people in England, they don't care about that sort of stuff; it is hard to shock people in that regard in England. Of course, if we'd been putting cats and dogs down, then we would have shocked some English people, but with Satan, you just get laughed at."

Which isn't to suggest that life was completely non-eventful in their homeland, where Sabbath were regularly threatened with hexes. On one occasion, they reportedly upset a Satanic group by refusing to appear at a "Night Of Satan" event at Stonehenge. Alex Sanders, England's "King of Witches" and a Sabbath fan, informed the band that the Satanists had placed a hex on each member. By now they were glad of their aluminium crosses.

But millions of better-adjusted fans applauded Black Sabbath as they rode the crest of a wave. *Master Of Reality* was a resounding triumph on both sides of the Atlantic after its release in August 1971, reaching number five in the UK and number eight in America.

It also completed a cycle. "*Master Of Reality* was the turning point," said Ozzy. "That was the last real Sabbath album, as far as I'm concerned."

The first and most innovative phase of the group's career was now over. They had written a trilogy of trailblazing albums, had completed the hat trick with producer Rodger Bain, had conquered the States, and had toured relentlessly.

Not bad for "four guys who couldn't even write our own names playing raw fucking music," as Ozzy saw it.

Now, though, it was time for them to get off the merry-go-round for a while.

They were exhausted, simply drained. They were also soaked with alcohol and frazzled with drugs, not least an escalating intake of cocaine.

And apart from all that, it was a chance for the newly married Ozzy to spend some time with his first wife, Thelma Riley, and his step-son Elliot.

It was also a chance for the productive "fifth member" to go off and find another band to infiltrate, having done what he or she set out to do for Black Sabbath.

Sweet Leaf

The track, and the album, open with the sounds of coughing, courtesy of Tony Iommi who had just

"I used to do a lot of grass and LSD back in the Black Sabbath days. One time I was out of my tree for a week talking to horses. And the weird thing was, they were talking back to me."

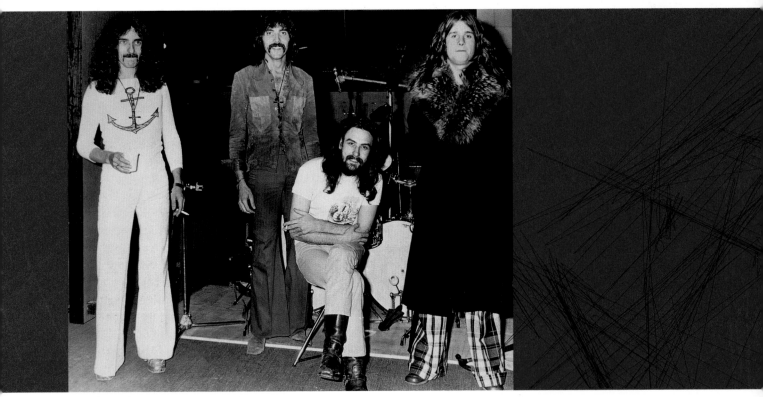

Ozzy: the scariest thing about him was his trousers

enjoyed a lengthy draw from a bong.

The band believed they owed it to the public to spread the good news about grass, and since "Sweet Leaf" was written for this specific purpose, Iommi's coughs erupted with perfect timing as the tapes began to roll.

Ozzy has described the origins of the song, which is heavily, densely unhurried and also noteworthy for a sensational guitar riff.

"I'd just come back from Dublin," said Ozzy, "and I had these Sweet Afton cigarettes you can only get in Ireland and it had on them, 'It's the sweetest leaf that you can taste.'

"Geezer wondered, 'What can we write this one about?' and I just looked at it and went, 'Sweet leaf – yeah!'"

Bill Ward talked about the track to Steven Rosen. He said: "That was very necessary to do at the time. Letting people know about marijuana – that's what it's about."

The lyrics take the form of a love song to the aromatic plant which, said Sabbath, was a cure-all. It could fill empty lives, lift depression and help its users feel "free" and "clear". In conclusion, the song urges: "Come on now, try it out/Straight people don't know what you're about."

This was a favourite of Ozzy, who carried on playing it live throughout his solo career. He recalled: "I used to do a lot of grass and LSD back in the Black Sabbath days. One time I was out of my tree for a week talking to horses. And the weird thing was, they were talking back to me."

More recently, he reflected: "I used to smoke all the time when I was younger. It seems to have become so strong nowadays – I hate the feeling. We used to smoke stuff that would make us giggle and give us the munchies. Now it's like being on acid – 'When's it gonna end?'"

after writing so voluminously about the dark side?

Some people believe that this, remarkably, was the case. Certainly, in all of his references to "After Forever", Butler has talked extremely seriously about the creative achievements of his lyric.

In contrast, there is nothing terribly sensitive about the track's big musical features, the crushing momentum and Iommi's enduring riff. One schoolboy rhyme follows another as Ozzy gives voice to Geezer's assertions that he had seen the truth and the light, had changed his ways and was certainly not about to join the lost souls who are "lonely and scared at the end of our days". He goes on to lambast those unfortunates who fail to realize that "God is the only way to love", or who are afraid to invite ridicule by acknowledging this. Finally, thunders the song: "I think it was true it was people like you/That crucified Christ".

"Isn't all this Christian folderol just the flip side of the Luciferian creed they commenced with and look back on balefully in 'Lord Of This World'?" queried *Rolling Stone*'s Lester Bangs.

In a work titled "Satanism and Heavy Metal: The Confusion Continues", author Matt C Paradise proposed: "Ozzy Osbourne, then lead singer for the band, could have very well been the first Christian rocker. Within the lyrics of their songs, they expressed Christian concepts of (the Christian) God vs Satan (Black Sabbath), reconciliation with Christian beliefs ('After Forever'), a plea to Jesus for help (a common theme in Sabbath songs, most notably 'The Thrill Of It All'), Satan being the motivator for war ('War Pigs') and many others.

"Of course, Sabbath also sang about degenerate, hippie topics as well, but even hippies have a love for master/slave relationships (drugs and Christian God being two of them)."

Avoiding the tricky topic of master/slave relationships, writer George Starostin ventured: "The fact that bassist Geezer Butler's lyrics were ultimately shallow, stupid, banal and even ridiculous, and, above all, were mostly directed against Satan – though it took some time to understand it – didn't help (the band). Even when they made the lyrics sound Christian, they were still treated as a new, horrendous brand of anti-Christs."

He added: "I have absolutely no doubt that these lyrics were totally tongue-in-cheek, attempted as a joke in the face of the church."

The last word goes to Ozzy, Geezer's mouthpiece for "After Forever", stating firmly in 1990: "I believe in God. I don't believe in the devil. I am not a devil worshipper. My kids do not sleep in the attic, hanging upside down on rafters."

After Forever

Geezer Butler's ode to Christianity did little to extricate Black Sabbath from their devilish associations, if that was indeed his intention. It simply managed to upset more people – the church authorities, who condemned it as blasphemous, and the Satanic community, who contended that Sabbath had sold out to God!

Still, it sent out a confusing message to fans, still arguing the contradictions. Had Geezer penned a supremely ironic dismissal of organized religion or was this some sort of spiritual insurance policy for a band beset by death threats and evil spells? Had he written, fictitiously or factually, of someone else's experience, in the first person? Was he opening a debate? Was he mixing it? Or was he really a God-fearing individual who felt it was time to bear witness, to set the record straight

CHILDREN OF THE GRAVE

Despite its gruesome title, the surging, riff-driven "Children Of The Grave" holds out a certain, Lennon-esque optimism and declares a war on evil. It calls upon the young generation to grow up resisting the xenophobia of their parents' world and to fight for peace and a future free of conflict and nuclear aggression until "love comes flowing through".

"Show the world that love is still alive!" counsels Ozzy, before issuing a stark, concluding warning: "You must be brave/Or you children of today are children of the grave/Yeah!"

The singer later shared his views of the song: "My interpretation of that is that in every generation, there's a new revolution. Every generation hates something about the current generation. It was our punk song, if you like."

LORD OF THIS WORLD

"That was our one and only Satan song," declared Geezer Butler, conveniently overlooking a goodly proportion of Black Sabbath's repertoire. "It's about old Nick."

Old Nick was treated to a suitable Sabbath work-out, one of those murderously slow–paced spectaculars like "Sweet Leaf", that moves from one mood to another with showers of showmanship from Tony Iommi and outbursts of spontaneous jamming. A continuing fan favourite, "Lord Of This World" is as short on lyrics as it is long on musical theatrics.

"Lord of this world, evil possessor/Lord of this world, he's your confessor now," sings Ozzy in his final summation.

INTO THE VOID

Again putting some distance between themselves and the morbid, macabre and occult obsessions for which they had become notorious, Black Sabbath returned to the themes they had visited on "Children Of The Grave", rejecting the wars, bigotry, brainwashing, wickedness and pollution of the world and proposing an escape by rocket ship to a place where "love is there to stay". "Leave the earth to Satan and his slaves/Leave them to their future in the grave!" cries Ozzy in the rip-roaring "Into The Void". Lyrically as well as musically, Sabbath were clearly ready to move on.

Other tracks on the album are the tiny instrumentals "Embryo" and "Orchid", and the hypnotic, despairing ballad "Solitude", arranged with flutes and echo.

VOL. 4

"The wonder and beauty of Black Sabbath...
how many shitting, hard, fucked-up times
I have been able to just cut my way through
with the help of Black Sabbath."
HENRY ROLLINS

It was all about drugs.

As Ozzy famously recalled: "When we did that album, it was like one big Roman orgy – we'd be in the jacuzzi all day doing coke, and every now and then we'd get up and do a song."

Sabbath had relocated to LA, theoretically to relax and record what would become *Vol. 4* at the Record Plant. In fact, a whole new world of temptation opened up to Ozzy's "dimbos from Birmingham", despite the fact that he and Thelma would have a daughter that year, Jessica (they would have a son, Louis, in 1975).

"We'd got the rock-star fever by then," Ozzy admitted. "Limousines everywhere, groupies sucking our dicks, dealers dropping by with bags of white powder."

Add to that an oceanic supply of booze and the scene was set for a wholesale slide into various addictions, a splintering of the old team spirit – and an album that somehow survived the chaos to return Black Sabbath to the charts with integrity and broadened ambition.

Ozzy's commitment to alcohol and cocaine was absolute, but he could seemingly take or leave his new bevy of female admirers, especially the strange ones who wanted to save his soul. But they weren't all like that.

"Groupies are great fun at first," confided a young Ozzy in 1976. "But then it gets a little bit tiring. You fuck maybe nine or ten of them, then one day you say, 'Leave me alone, I'm human, I've got feelings.' I've had them, I've fucked them off. I'm not saying I'm a goody-goody… we used to have all-night parties and line them up. But you got to sleep, you got to eat."

You got to record, too.

The big plan for *Vol 4* was variety. After three uncompromisingly hard-line albums, the band and their co-producer Patrick Meehan set out to introduce some lighter strokes, a more dramatic sense of dynamics

within the songs and a clearer definition between them. That they succeeded, given the worldly distractions and the reported arguments between the band and their production team, was a triumph in itself.

The balance was just about right. There was a certain cohesion, a sense that the tracks logically fitted together while, at the same time, not stifling the megaforce of vintage Sabbath, their riffs and rumbles and Ozzy's trademark, macabre shriek, which could give way at any moment to the percussive peculiarity of "FX", the

acoustic, instrumental sensitivity of "Laguna Sunrise" or the speeding guitar thrash of "Supernaut".

Sabbath finally discovered an interest in studio technology, became increasingly melodic and made a deliberate attempt at brevity, with several songs clocking in closer to the three-minute mark than the eight minutes of the opening track, "Wheels Of Confusion". Yet the pervading atmosphere was thick and cheerless.

Lyrically, the group turned their collective back on the influences of old. Gone are the swords and sorcery, the demons, devils and hellish visions of Geezer Butler's nightmare imagination. In their place are earthbound songs that describe what was going on at the time with Black Sabbath – in their hearts, in their heads and up their noses.

Naturally, there was a degree of resistance to all of this from the more inflexible fans who wanted anything but change or progress. Still, there was plenty of metal mayhem to satisfy the vast majority of the audience, and just enough diversity to make things interesting and to prove that Ozzy and the gang were not a one-dimensional band. The album, released in the autumn of 1972, crashed into the UK chart at number eight and in America, at number 13.

There are those who feel, in retrospect, that the success of *Vol. 4* was regrettable since it vindicated the band's new-found desire to experiment and thus encouraged them in later years to stray even further from their original formula – with less convincing results.

It's clear that Ozzy had his reservations about the album, even though he publicly endorsed its "richer" musical flavour. He also at this time described Black Sabbath as "the tightest friendship thing I've ever encountered," which wasn't strictly true either.

Stresses and strains were beginning to surface in the relationships amid the mountains of cocaine, rivers of booze and whispers of power-games in the studio, with Tony Iommi said to be dominating the recordings. (To be fair to Iommi, the leader's role had been thrust upon him some time before by bandmates who were happy to leave him alone, composing, while they jollied it up in the nearest pub.)

Ozzy's relationship with Geezer Butler pre-dated Black Sabbath. It had its stormy periods but always levelled out eventually. With Iommi, however, the atmosphere was different. Quoted by Steven Rosen, Ozzy admitted: "Tony Iommi and I never really were very close. I went to school with Tony and I was in a band with Tony, but we never really socialized too often… he always had a barrier around him. I never, ever really knew him."

But the most serious upset happened when the rest of the group invited drummer Bill Ward literally to leave the building.

CHANGES

The album kicks in with the epic "Wheels Of Confusion", an unorthodox amalgamation of changing tempos, solos and a simply monumental riff from Tony Iommi, while the following, powerful "Tomorrow's Dream", much shorter and certainly more mainstream, was released as a single, the first since "Paranoid", to little excitement in the chart. So far, so Sabbath.

But three tracks in, they rang some "Changes". Tinkling piano keys underpin a hugely melodic and emotional performance from Ozzy as the band weaves an irresistible air of melancholy to create what has been pinpointed as the world's first power ballad.

Like the two songs which precede it, "Changes" is an unhappy proposition, a simplistic story of lost love and regret: "Wish I could go back and change these years".

The unidentified break-up (rumoured in some circles

to describe Bill Ward's first divorce) is attributed to the wicked ways of the world – a possible reference to the life of wine, women and song that the band were living during their big Hollywood adventure.

It's a track that has sharply divided long-time Sabbath fans. Some would like to write it out of the history books forever; others contend that it remains the loveliest song they've ever heard from the band.

Supernaut

No complaints here, as Sabbath weigh in with a hectic energy that finds Tony Iommi playing hard and fast in what is probably his first recorded instance of thrash guitar riffing. The sheer magnitude of the song, the combination of juggernaut aggression and catchy hooks – plus a drum solo! – puts "Supernaut" up there among the tracks most loved by fans to this day.

It's generally interpreted as a drug song, a selfishly worded defence of some illegal substance. It could be about acid – the assertion that "I want to touch the sun/But I don't need to fly" is not the only fanciful pronouncement. It could be about heroin, the wares of a "distant man" seen to be hovering around the lyrics waving a spoon. And, of course, it could be about cocaine, just because of the superhuman assurance pervading the lyric and because we know how devotedly the members of Black Sabbath adored their white stuff in the good old days of 1972.

Flying in the face of their Satanic reputation and the ambiguous, Christian sentiments of "After Forever", the song starkly decrees, "Got no religion, don't need no friends", a theme which would recur, in greater detail, later on in the album to compound the mysteries of Black Sabbath's spiritual soap opera.

remove the offending word, he nevertheless smuggled it on to the recording by means of a whisper, determined to immortalize a lifestyle that revolved around coke while at the same time admitting to journalists that he thought he was "going nuts".

He said recently, "I remember that when you'd run out of cocaine, you'd be scratching the carpet for anything that resembled the white stuff. It could be dog shit and you'd be putting it up your nose: 'Oh, look, there's a rock!'"

Matter-of-factly, he stated: "We were doing tons of the fucking stuff."

While the group storm into the song like the undisputed heavyweight champions they were, changing pace with a bruising and unsmiling authority, Ozzy gives forth in a stark, almost chanting vocal about the satisfying numbness of "Feeling happy in my vein/Icicles within my brain". The lyrics speak of a strange and self-contained comfort, but the imagery is largely cold and lonely – not the most persuasive argument for a new hobby – and a defiant tone again enters: "Don't tell me that it's doing me wrong/You're the one who's really a loser…" These days, Ozzy would probably disagree with the sentiment, while defending to the death his right to have sung it.

SNOWBLIND

This was to be the name of the LP before yet another intervention from the record label. With the decision to add an upside-down cross to the artwork for *Black Sabbath*, executives had aimed to heighten the band's notoriety. But in forbidding "War Pigs" as a title for the album eventually called *Paranoid* and by then banning "Snowblind", the boardroom flexed some serious, censorious muscle: Sabbath were being firmly guided away from controversy.

"Snowblind" – an unequivocal reference to cocaine – was axed in favour of the anaemic title *Vol. 4*.

There was no huge revolt from the band, but they did strike back with a couple of blows against the empire. The sleeve acknowledgements thank the "COKE-Cola" company. And Ozzy blurted out "cocaine" at the end of every verse of the "Snowblind" track. Ordered to

CORNUCOPIA

Geezer Butler was spurred into action by a radio report that "only" 25 men had been killed in the Vietnam war that week. Seizing upon "cornucopia" as a keyword for abundance and prosperity, his lyrics bitterly attacked society's consumerism and heartlessness. It was all very admirable: a band with a conscience.

But back in the early Seventies, when first-division heavy metal was a place of unparalleled excess and self-indulgence, it seems hypocritical for any rock star to criticize the expensive habits of others.

Sex, drugs and rock'n'roll could well be said to be the group's own equivalent of the "Little toys, fast sports cars and motor noise" so scathingly highlighted in the song, and for all of his good intentions, Geezer's focus on symbols rather than symptoms rang hollow, especially since Black Sabbath were in just as much of a "plastic place" as those criticized in his lyrics.

"I remember that when you'd run out of cocaine, you'd be scratching the carpet for anything that resembled the white stuff."

'These boots aren't made for walkin'...'

Little of this was of any interest to Bill Ward, whose problems with "Cornucopia" were closer to home. He loathed the track, which is a heavy-duty Sabbath rocker, loaded with time and tempo changes, and Bill could not get to grips with the patterns. The band returned to England to finish up some bits and pieces for the album, "Cornucopia" among them. Bill was on booze and coke round the clock, was fed up in the studio, and was developing a mental block, a "terrible resentment" about "Cornucopia".

Something about Bill's friendship with Alvin Lee was also causing friction in the ranks. Ward's bandmates – including his usual ally, Ozzy – unanimously decided that he should go home, since he wasn't serving any useful purpose in the studio. Unfortunately, Bill didn't have a home to go to, since he'd been on the road so much, he hadn't reckoned he needed one. Bill trudged off into the night with his wife, profoundly shocked and fearful for his job. The pair gravitated to Geezer Butler's house and spent the night sleeping under coats in his back garden.

"That was the very first indication that there was a change, because that had never happened before," said Ward to Steven Rosen. "It had all been fine. Suddenly, here in *Vol. 4* there was a change, a definite change.

"It really scared me. And it was the first time that any band member had ever been rebuked. It hurt. I mean, they didn't want me in the studio. Sometimes we'd have cross words, but that was the first time I actually felt like I'd blown it." Eventually, Ward completed his drum part to everyone's satisfaction.

Under The Sun

The chunky guitar riffs, the solos, the drum fills and the thrill of Ozzy in full flight conform to the original Sabbath blueprint. But the lyrics utter a complete rejection of everything that had gone before.

"Well I don't want no demon to tell me what it's all about…" Geezer didn't want no black magician either, or no preacher telling him about God. He didn't want to know about the afterlife, and he didn't want to know the vast majority of his fellow-human beings. "I just believe in myself," he wrote, "Cos no one else is true."

If the lyrics are to be taken literally, this all appears to have arisen from some drug-induced revelation: he had opened the door, he assured us. He had released his mind, realized that life was "one big overdose" and decided that from then on, he would follow his own path and to hell with everyone else.

It must have been one of those moments; a more familiar Geezer would re-emerge on the next Black Sabbath album.

Other tracks on the album are the oddly experimental, some might say dispensable "FX", which runs to just over a minute and a half; the instrumental "Laguna Sunrise", with its acoustic guitars and string section; and the battering "St Vitus Dance", an unusual, new take on the age-old story of women chasing rock stars for their money.

SABBATH BLOODY SABBATH

"I was always more of a feminine person when I was young.
Then when my hormones started swinging around
and I started getting facial hair, I had to
let off my male steam somewhere. So I started
smoking pot and listening to
Black Sabbath and Black Flag..."
KURT COBAIN, NIRVANA

"I love Black Sabbath.
They made an amazing contribution
to music today. Almost every band that
made it big in the Nineties owes a
debt to them"
DAVE GROHL, NIRVANA

The whole Satanism thing was a big surprise for us when we came to America. They received death threats, were ordered to deter... their music to mayors and police departments nervous about letting the gigs go ahead, had shows called off, were cheered in LA by members of Charles Manson's "family", and in San Francisco, had a procession held in their honour by Anton La Vey, high priest of the Church of Satan.

With *Vol. 4*, Black Sabbath had stuck their necks out, but record sales showed that the fans supported their attempts at diversification. Reassured, they intended to widen their musical horizons still further.

It seemed logical, then, that by returning to Los Angeles, they could recreate the circumstances which had produced *Vol. 4*, but things didn't go according to plan. Walking into their usual studio at the Record Plant, they were confronted by a newly installed synthesizer – a big and terrifying monster that ruined the cosy familiarity of their home from home. The machine was a harbinger of things to come, but those things would not happen in LA.

Tony Iommi – whose riffs, seemingly plucked from the air, were the starting point for almost every great Sabbath song – went down with a serious case of writer's block, a condition which afflicts him to this day.

He said recently: "You do get a block. You can't just constantly be creative every minute of the day. You've got to come up against obstacles where you can't think or you can't play. Sometimes I can't pick up the guitar – I can't play it, I don't want to play it. Usually, I want to play it when I'm somewhere that I haven't got it. Inspiration just comes at times when maybe you are more relaxed."

By now, Ozzy, Geezer and Bill were used to following Iommi's lead, and they depended on him to the point that they rarely brought any original ideas to the studio – a fact which the brooding guitarist was coming to resent more and more, and which added to the tensions simmering beneath the surface of the band.

As recently as 1996, he admitted: "I've gone through so many problems in my own personal life because of Sabbath, because I'm the one sitting there night and day in a studio, working on this stuff. And it's taken up a major part of my life, and consequently it's upset my married life. So it's been annoying…"

He also said, "Everything's gone by the wayside over the years for the band."

With Iommi searching in vain for inspiration and receiving no back-up, Black Sabbath floundered: they could make no headway with the album. Conceding defeat, they packed up their troubles and returned to England for a rest.

Inspirationally, they chose to regroup in a creepy old castle in the wilds of Wales, where they plugged in – of course - in the dungeons. It was a productive but hair-raising experience. Black Sabbath, much-vaunted lords of the underworld and devil's disciples, were too scared to stay overnight in the castle. Instead, they drove miles

Sabbath bloody Sabbath: death walks behind you... and in front of you

every day, there and back, to sleep in the safety of their own beds. Naturally, it was a haunted castle.

Iommi told Steven Rosen: "Ozzy and I were walking from the rehearsal room towards the armoury, where they had their weapons and stuff, and we saw this guy coming down, dressed in black. He just went into this door... and we both sort of looked at each other and said, 'Who the hell was that?'

"Nobody else was in the castle, apart from us and the people who owned it. So we went into this room to see who it was and there was nobody else there, and there was no other way out..." The property owners confirmed the next day that Iommi and Ozzy had stumbled across the resident ghost, and advised them that there was really nothing to worry about.

The Hammer Horror atmosphere of their new surroundings was perfect; it worked wonders for the group. Iommi's creative juices began to flow, and the

Ozzy: blinded by the light

songs that would form the body of *Sabbath Bloody Sabbath* took shape without any further impediment.

Producing the album themselves, the band began to overcome their initial techno-fear and to embrace the beast that had threatened them so dramatically in California: the synthesizer. Calling on the services of Rick Wakeman, master keyboardist with progressive kings Yes, they turned out an album that was noteworthy for its tunefulness, keyboards and synthesized effects and for the organ sounds that Iommi was coaxing from his guitar with a phaser. Sabbath were less bothered than ever before about the blustering riffs and relentless, grinding weight of their tradition, although there was a partial return to the other-worldly topics of yesteryear.

Sabbath Bloody Sabbath was the sequel to *Vol. 4* and even more of a gamble, musically, but the fans proved their solidarity with wads of banknotes. It rushed to number four in Britain after its release at the end of 1973, and it enjoyed a US placing of number 11 after the New Year.

But time has not been quite so kind to the album. Approaching 30 years later, Sabbath buffs are known to huff over its levity, and its friends and foes alike are almost unanimous that it could have done without the weak instrumental "Fluff" and Ozzy's first, fully-fledged composition, "Who Are You?" To others, *Sabbath Bloody Sabbath* remains a great rock milestone, a testament to the band's adventuring spirit and willingness to depart from a tried-and-tested formula. Back then, though, Sabbath themselves had decided that enough was enough: they had followed their wanderlust far enough, and now it was time to get back to basics.

But could they? Drink and drugs were wreaking havoc within the group, and Bill Ward had almost reached the point of no return. Lucky to be alive today, the clean-living Ward confesses that, "I was really diminished by my narcotics use," having lost the dynamic drive that a world-class band should be able to depend on from the drummer.

And then there was Ozzy. Hell-bent on satisfying a gargantuan appetite for whatever lotions and potions came his way, he was nevertheless aware of a niggling little voice in his head which told him that something didn't feel right around here. Rumours began to circulate that he was leaving. He denied them all, although he was indeed beginning to think about a life without the band. It would just take time to make the break. He later admitted: "The beginning of the end for me came after *Sabbath Bloody Sabbath*." And he revealed: "I wasn't prepared to own up to the rest of the band. I didn't want to give up the success and recognition."

Sabbath Bloody Sabbath

This was the song that smashed Iommi's writer's block as the group reassembled in the Welsh castle. "I just started this riff," he said, "and then they started up, and it worked well."

Allegedly named after a headline in the late, lamented British music weekly *Melody Maker*, it is quintessential Sabbath, a detuned, riffing dirge whose fearsome weight lifts only slightly to create contrasting moments. It blew the cobwebs away from around the band and the dark corners of their dungeon, giving rise to a new outpouring of ideas.

Said Ozzy: "The title track was something about the word 'God' and changing it all around. Instead of 'God bless all of you,' it was 'Bog blast all of you.' Geezer Butler wrote those words and he was very fucking stoned. He must have been."

Sabbath analysts have suggested that Geezer's lyrics betray a weariness and a suspicion of the phenomenon surrounding Black Sabbath – an opinion backed by Bill Ward. Geezer wrote: "Dreams turn to nightmares, heaven turns to hell/Burned out confusion, nothing more to tell."

The bass player, however, has reported especially happy memories of making the album. Talking to writer John Stix in 1994 with Tony Iommi, he said: "Right before that, we were in a terrible slump. We were all exhausted from touring. We weren't getting on very well. Then Tony came up with the riff for 'Sabbath Bloody Sabbath' and everybody sparked into life. The year while we were doing that was a really good year, personally. I'll always remember that album and look back on it with a good feeling."

Indeed, he stated that of all of the Ozzy-era albums, it was the one he would urge fans to rediscover, citing the title track as a personal favourite. "It was a whole new era for us," continued Geezer. "We felt really open on that album. It was a great atmosphere, good time, great coke! Just like a new birth for me."

Tony Iommi agreed: "There are some great tracks on that album. It was a great feeling from rehearsals to writing to recording. It was just a great time. That was a good album for me. I enjoyed that."

"We felt really open on that album. It was a great atmosphere, good time, great coke!"

A National Acrobat

"That was just me thinking about who selects what sperm gets through the egg," explained Geezer Butler, off-handedly.

And it's just as well he did, because no one else would have guessed it. "When little worlds collide/I'm trapped inside my embryonic cell," sang Ozzy, broadcasting Geezer's mysterious allusions to the wriggling failures and the unborn child that was never conceived.

From there on in, there's lots of talk about the seeds, the secret, the soul and the life beyond. It would appear that the text deliberately widens to represent something bigger, something human, to urge the audience to make the most of their time on earth, and to state a belief in survival, in some form, beyond death.

There again, Geezer may simply have decided in a moment of madness that sperm have souls, that they might be reincarnated along with everyone else or welcomed into the eternal kingdoms of heaven and hell.

Fans applauded "A National Acrobat", dwelling on its diverse musical power and Iommi's affecting guitar riff, although one reviewer appealed: "The subject matter of the song is not quite clear to me. Does anyone know?" And another ventured: "I get the idea that this song is about someone who has seen the world and knows all that life has to offer."

Who are you?

Not even distantly related to the Who track of the same name, this was the first real song that Ozzy ever wrote. It's the album's big synthesizer track, and one which has stood the test of time very badly as far as Sabbath fans are concerned.

Quoted by Steven Rosen, Ozzy had this to say: "I dig singing the spacey things with electronics. I dig this emptiness thing. The synthesizer gives this empty feeling of depth and distance. It's like forever.

"Like 'Who Are You?' I wrote that in the kitchen while my wife was cooking some food. I had a synthesizer on the table and I was just fucking about with a tape machine and it just came out…

"I never played instruments. I don't even know what the fuck I played. I really don't know what key or chord or what notes I played. It's just the sound."

"Please, I beg you, tell me, in the name of hell, who are you? Who are you?" implores Ozzy as the song reaches its conclusion.

Determinedly non-muso in his new capacity as a writer, Ozzy was nevertheless lambasted, not so much for his nasal vocals but for his very nerve in allowing his firstborn song to be interpreted and accompanied by a machine.

"We were never afraid to do whatever we felt at the time," replied Geezer Butler. "I think that's what kept us as Black Sabbath. Listen to anything past the first three albums – we do soul stuff, not what everybody else would do, but there's funky bass lines in there or funky guitar bits, some synthesizers, and straight-ahead ballads ("Changes"). Anything. We felt it would kill the band if we weren't allowed to grow up within it."

Tony Iommi enthused: "Rick Wakeman, who played on 'Who Are You?', was great, really great. He was wild back then. We took Yes on tour with us, and brought them to America on their first tour. But Rick used to travel with us and not Yes for some reason."

Spiral Architect

Ozzy Osbourne thinks of Geezer Butler when he thinks of "Spiral Architect".

"Geezer's an incredible lyricist," said Ozzy. "Not many people know he wrote 90 per cent (Butler would say 95 per cent) of the lyrics for Sabbath. I'll never forget when he wrote the lyrics to 'Spiral Architect'. I was on the phone and I asked him if he had the lyrics for me to sing yet.

"He says to me, 'Got a pen?' He started off, 'Sorcerers of madness, selling me their time…' And I go, 'You're fucking reading this out of a book. You're joking!' My mouth dropped open." Geezer, clearly still fascinated by

"Please, I beg you, tell me, in the name of hell, who are you?"

human creation, explained: "It was about life's experiences being added to a person's DNA to create a unique individual."

At its close, the song decides, optimistically, "Of all the things I value most of all/I look upon my earth and feel the warmth/And know that it is good." Sabbath were gradually changing their tune, reaching for the positive while recognizing and documenting the opposite forces.

"Spiral Architect", described by one critic as a "philosophical symphony", remains one of the album's stand-out tracks with its ambitious but confident electric/acoustic combinations, keyboards and string effects.

Other tracks on the album are "Fluff", a much maligned, sluggish and layered instrumental deemed too long for its own good; "Sabbra Cadabra", a shag-happy slice of rock'n'roll adorned by keyboards; the highly rated and grungy "Killing Yourself To Live", with its building tempos and guitar solo; and the sturdy "Looking For Today", which is carried up to the very edges of pop melody by a repeating riff augmented by handclaps, keyboards and a flute arrangement.

SABOTAGE

"I discovered Black Sabbath
by digging through my older brother's record
collection. Their album covers really drew me in.
I immediately thought, 'I gotta put this on.' And when
I did, I couldn't believe it. It was like,
'Whoa!' Heavy as shit.
Sabbath was everything that the
Sixties weren't. Their music was so cool
because it was completely anti-hippie."

JAMES HETFIELD,
METALLICA

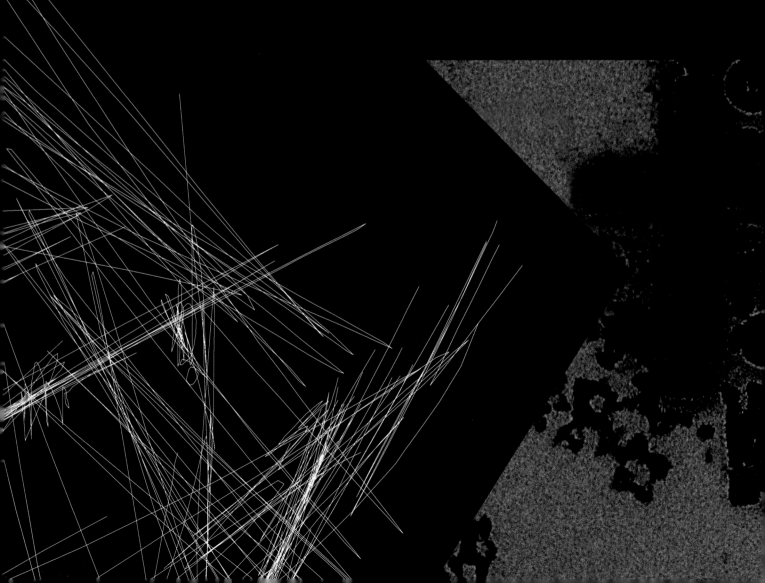

Metallica – inspired by the heavy, heavy monster sound of Sabbath

Everything should have been just beautiful. Black Sabbath were ideally poised to partake of everything good that the world had to offer. But *Sabotage* said otherwise.

Tony Iommi explained: "Every album we did had a little story behind it, something good you'd remember, or something bad at that time, different things you're going through. I remember the *Sabotage* album was one…

"That was a terrible period for us because we were getting bloody lawsuits in the studio. People were delivering us writs and stuff. That's why there's a song called 'The Writ' on it."

Typically to the point, Ozzy declared: "By the time we did *Sabotage*, we were all fucked up with drugs." He went on to talk of financial disputes and management clashes which would come to a head in a welter of recriminations and flying legal documents during the sessions for the album.

After parting company with Jim Simpson, the band had signed up to a management deal with industry faces Wilf Pine and Patrick Meehan (the latter claiming a co-production credit on *Vol. 4*). Now, the band were ready for another change. They tried managing themselves for a short while before signing up to Don Arden – ironically, a former employer of Meehan and Pine.

While Arden managed the band, his daughter Sharon worked as the company receptionist. Legend has it that when Sharon first clapped eyes on Ozzy – her future husband – she was terrified, shocked by the tap he wore round his neck and his insistence on sitting on the floor rather than in a chair. Such was her horror that she tried to persuade another staffer to bring him a cup of tea, so as to avoid having to serve it herself. Ozzy and Sharon didn't know it at the time, but she would be his passport to a successful solo career and, eventually, the reason that he lived rather than died from his addiction to drink and drugs.

It was still on Ozzy's mind that he should leave Black Sabbath. Despite his professions of pride in *Sabotage* at the time, his musical visions were increasingly at odds with Iommi's. While the guitarist was looking towards a more mature expression of his musical talents, Ozzy wanted to keep the old flag flying for the gods of thunder, and he showed his dissatisfaction by retreating from the recording process. Where once he would have been in the thick of things, improvising over the top of whatever twists and turns the band was taking, now he was staying out of it, usually only reporting in to sing his designated parts.

'Let's hear it for Toni Iommi and his fantastic legs..."

Tony Iommi has since pointed to other weaknesses in the formerly solid foundations of the group. With money no object, and the band surrounded by all the status symbols of their wealth, the houses, the expensive cars, the chauffeur-driven limos, the brand new musical equipment and the gofer with the suitcase full of coke, Iommi felt the band were losing their edge, their hunger. And although they were heroes around the world, they still received little encouragement from the press.

"Millions of people loved us, but millions of people hated us as well," said Iommi. "A lot of journalists hated the sight of us. I think we became the band they liked to pick on from day one, because we'd gone against all the things we were supposed to be."

With all of these negative energies lurking in the background to the sessions, *Sabotage* – the band's first UK album release for NEMS, although they remained with Warner Bros in America – somehow emerged unscathed. It fused the archetypal, earthquaking sound of the Sabbath with some lighter strokes, in a full-scale production job by the band and Mike Butcher. Although the album featured keyboards, played by Gerald Woodruffe, who also accompanied them on tour, it didn't have the awkward, self-conscious

experimentation of the previous albums.

"*Sabotage* is not only Black Sabbath's best record since *Paranoid*, it might be their best ever," raved *Rolling Stone*'s Billy Altman. "Even with the usual themes of death, destruction and mental illness running throughout this album, the unleashed frenzy and raw energy they've returned to here comes like a breath of fresh air."

Ozzy was in a state of confusion when the recordings, in Morgan Studios, London, and Brussels, were finally complete.

"I had heard so much of it that I had to leave it alone for some time. When I heard it again, I *hated* it. I realized that because of the constant work on it, I'd built this barrier in my head, but I'm really satisfied now."

He elaborated: "To me, *Sabotage* beats the last album (*Sabbath Bloody Sabbath*) – but I still have a liking for the last one... We had got into the studio production thing and it takes a couple of albums to get into that. You go through all the experiments of banging dustbin lids and running herds of cattle through the studio..."

One thing Ozzy really did abhor was the "horrible" sleeve photo, in which he and Bill Ward were quite unusually dressed. "Bill has got his wife's tights on with my checked underpants underneath and I'm dressed up

like a homo in a kimono. But you've got to understand the times – it was the Seventies, there was no MTV, no one to guide us..."

For all of his misgivings about his future with the band, Ozzy has reported some enjoyable memories from the recordings.

"Every time there was a session we used to call it Chapter 99 – 'Will Black Sabbath complete the album this time?' It was like a bizarre nightmare sometimes but other times it was fun, especially the times we started throwing custard pies at each other."

The band were rewarded not with custard pies but with a number seven chart entry in the UK and a number 28 placing in the US after its release in September 1975.

Hole In The Sky/Symptom Of The Universe

Blasting the album into life, "Hole In The Sky" and "Symptom Of the Universe" together announced that Sabbath were back in business. The headbanging "Hole In The Sky" – once memorably described as "music to demolish buildings by" – was deliberately chosen as the

first track because of its barbarously simple rock formula: no keyboards, no flights of fancy. It was a statement of intent.

On Geezer Butler's part, it was a statement of something else. And, no, he wasn't prophesying any problems with the ozone layer. According to Tony Iommi, Geezer's lyrics dwelled on "sort of a universal thing. It's basically about the astral plane."

Taking the chance to cock a snook at the "dogs of war" – arguably a reference to the hated "war pigs" – and again attack the greed and affluence of the West, Geezer turned in a typically spacey lyric in which he was "seeing nowhere through the eyes of a lie".

In the most gloriously incomprehensible couplet, he confides: "The synonyms of all the things that I've said/Are just the riddles that are built in my head."

Linking "Hole In The Sky" to "Symptom Of The Universe" is the 49-second, acoustic guitar snippet, "Don't Start (Too Late)". Tony Iommi told Steven Rosen: "The way we came about that was the engineer was a comical chap and he kept saying, 'Don't start! Don't start!' But it was too late, because we had started."

Shattering these fragile moments, Sabbath storm back loud and proud, Ozzy screaming like the banshee of his reputation and Iommi knocking out another of his killer riffs, with "Symptom Of The Universe". A lengthy track, it plunges dramatically from the savage attack of its first few minutes to a laid-back and jazzy conclusion with Iommi on acoustic guitar.

Journeying again through time and space, the lyrics pour out theories about love, rebirth, eternity and the universe, ending on a brightly optimistic note: "We'll find happiness together in the summer skies of love".

McGalomania

Considered by many Sabbath fans to be both the centrepiece and the masterpiece of *Sabotage*, the unsettling "Megalomania" checks in at almost 10 minutes.

It builds theatrically, compellingly, from a starting point of subtle, acoustic restraint into a riot of multi-riffing guitar that bangs out rounds of hostile fire and feedback as Ozzy rises up to denounce the god who had for so long imprisoned and persecuted Geezer Butler, or the character he had created.

> "Love wouldn't go with the style of music we play. It would be like going to see *Frankenstein* with the *Sound Of Music* soundtrack behind it."

Once asked to explain the song, Tony Iommi confessed to being no more qualified than anybody else to decipher the lyrics. "It's hard to quite explain that number,' he chuckled. 'Geezer wrote the words...'"

Whether it was the Biblical God, the god of darkness or even the god of success, desire, love or cocaine, its hold was something that Geezer's hero "could not control". The words describe a life of shame and sorrow, in which the protagonist emerges from the shadows to square up to some hefty, personal demon, at the same time fighting schizophrenia and the knowledge that he was liable to slip at any moment.

"I've seized my soul in the fires of hell/Peace of mind eluded me, but now it's all mine," wails Ozzy, intermittently urging the tormenting power, "Why don't

A moment of reflection

you just get out of my life, yeah?"

Ozzy commented at the time about the general nature of Sabbath lyrics: "They're not downer lyrics, they're just telling everybody where it's at. That's all it is. People must think we sleep off rafters with wings on our backs every night, taking reds and drinking wine. We see a lot and we write about what we see...

"Love wouldn't go with the style of music we play. It would be like going to see *Frankenstein* with the *Sound Of Music* soundtrack behind it."

Supertzar

Although *Sabotage* is primarily an all-out, hard rock album, written to be played live onstage, it does have its moments of light relief and diversion – memorably with the instrumental "Supertzar".

Here, Black Sabbath were joined by the full English Chamber Choir, arranged by Will Malone, who provided an unearthly counterbalance to Iommi's dedicated riffing. Indeed, there are those who feel that the idea could have

Having a headbanger's ball

stretched to create a full-blown, operatic, metal anthem.

Iommi recently stated: "It was a thing we said years ago when we did 'Laguna Sunrise' and 'Supertzar' with the choir – we went out to do what we liked. We played what we enjoyed."

"It sounds like one of those epic, bloody *Ben Hur* themes," countered Ozzy.

He later claimed: "I remember being stuck in Miami with no dough during this album. We called the label to get more money and they sent us a telegram saying, 'Don't worry – the hamburgers are on the way.' Sick fucking joke. It wasn't a happy time, although when Tony came up with the riff to 'Supertzar', it fucking pinned my ears back. I was *gobsmacked*."

Am I Going Insane (Radio)

Described by Tony Iommi as "a sort of Moog [synthesizer] guitar groove", this was clearly an emotional exercise for its author, Ozzy. He revealed in 1976: "Doing 'Am I Going Insane' exorcised the feelings in me. I don't think I'm going mad any more, but I'm still angry – I've *always* been angry."

Eerie atmospheres compound a lyric which talks, with fabulous déjà vu, of being paranoid and of being a "schizo brain". Seemingly, it encapsulated Ozzy's anxieties about his place in the world, and the fears that assailed him about staying in Sabbath and, also, about leaving them. Oh, and in case the bracketed "Radio" implies that there may be another edit – there isn't.

The Writ

This was the big, autobiographical moment; the group's eight-minute tirade against the music industry and its inherent ruthlessness. Spilling out all of the anger, dismay, defiance and bloodlust that they had felt during their management struggles and their enforced retreat into a stultifying legal quagmire, Black Sabbath were finally able to put the gloves on and retaliate.

"What kind of people do you think we are?" challenges Ozzy, as the track courses through its riff-riven changes. "Another joker who's a rock and roll star for you, just for you?"

Charged up with all the righteous fury of men with the moral high ground, individuals who had worked for and believed in the honour of rock'n'roll only to be repaid with lies, false promises and betrayal, Sabbath warn that they have transformed their hatred into a curse before eventually looking forward to a time when "everything is gonna work out fine".

It's probably the most direct lyric in their repertoire, and all the more chilling for it. Forget old red-eye crouching over there in the corner of your darkest nightmare: this is about real life and real people – the nightmare in your living room. "The Writ" is recommended listening for every would-be musician.

Other tracks on the album are "The Thrill Of It All", addressing "Mr Jesus" with feedback, moodswings and an unusual tendency to prog-rock, and the 23-second "Blow On A Jug", included on some original vinyl and cassette album copies. It was an informal and low-volume recording of Ozzy and Bill Ward larking about in the studio, à la Nitty Gritty Dirt Band, tacked onto the end of "The Writ" – the calm after the storm.

Never Say Die

"Everybody knows
that Black Sabbath started
everything, and almost
every single thing that people are playing today
has already been done
by Black Sabbath.
They wrote every single
good riff... ever."
ROB ZOMBIE,
WHITE ZOMBIE

Sabbath in unforgettable, Seventies fashion statement

With *Sabotage*, Ozzy had made his last great Sabbath album. Summing up their achievements in February 1976, the double-album compilation *We Sold Our Soul For Rock'n'Roll* neatly rounded off the most creative and influential phase of their career.

With *Technical Ecstasy*, released in October the same year and marking a return to Vertigo Records, they again departed from the familiar, ditching their dark and mystical soundstorms to explore other musical territories.

Produced by Black Sabbath and retaining Gerald Woodruffe on keyboards, the album roved from the string-laden ballad "She's Gone" through the gentle, country-flavoured "It's Alright", with Bill Ward on vocals, to the operatic dramas of "Gypsy".

Resisting the temptations of the paranormal, the lyrics focused resolutely on autobiography ("Back Street Kids"), relationships, prostitutes and that good old, cure-all, time-honoured fellow, the "Rock'n'Roll Doctor". A slice of down-home boogie, this was one of the album's rockier offerings. The fans' favourite, "Dirty Women", was harder still, and more than seven minutes long.

"I just didn't give a shit. I would go in there loaded every day, and in the end I felt guilty, 'cos I abused what we had."

But none of the tracks were particularly heavy, they weren't metal, and although the album charted at number 13 in the UK and 51 in the US, it left many fans disappointed. A solid enough recording, it didn't have a lot of spirit – certainly not by Sabbath standards.

Ozzy, again, did his duty for the press, but his PR routine was becoming transparent. "It was enjoyable to make," he said of *Technical Ecstasy*. "Well, Tony enjoyed it…" He continued: "It's like when the laxative has worked and you've just got it all out…"

Privately, he was disillusioned. Two years later, he said: "Why couldn't we be leaders any more? I'll tell you why. 'Cos we all became so content with it, so bored that we just got lazy, that's why. It seems to me that the names Black Sabbath and *Technical Ecstasy* were diametrically opposed to each other. Nobody thought about it. I just didn't give a shit. I would go in there loaded every day, and in the end I felt guilty, 'cos I abused what we had."

Ozzy quit the band.

He was replaced by singer Dave Ward, ex-Fleetwood Mac and Savoy Brown. During Ozzy's three-month lay-off, Jack Osbourne, his father, died. As if that weren't bad enough, Ozzy's plans for working with various other musicians foundered when he discovered the extent of their commercial obsessions.

"I missed the family atmosphere of Black Sabbath," he confessed, still raw from the loss of his father. "I had a rest, but knew in my heart that I was making a mistake and I just had to get back in there."

He explained: "It's been like a holiday. It's given me a lot of time to think, and although I'd been trying to work with other musicians, it was very difficult. After nine years with the same people, you get used to things. When they rang up to ask me if I'd come back, I knew there was only one answer."

Black Sabbath flew out to Canada's freezing winter to record *Never Say Die!* in a Toronto studio, where Ozzy refused to sing any of the material already written with Ward.

Tony Iommi told Steven Rosen: "That, to me, was an album that was very difficult. Particularly, it was very difficult for me to come up with the ideas and try putting them together that quick...

"We were all into silly games... We were in Toronto for something like five months. It was quite a long time, and we were getting really drugged out... We'd go down to the sessions and have to pack up because we were too stoned. Nobody could get anything right. We were all over the place. Everybody was playing a different thing."

Bill Ward admits that, "I was getting ill all the time with my drinking."

Geezer Butler was having problems with the lyric-writing. He said, "I used to hate doing it towards the end of the Ozzy era. He'd say, 'I'm not singing that.' So you'd have to rethink the whole thing."

Ozzy recalled: "The reason we'd gone to Canada was because of the tax exile thing, because the taxes are so high in England. In the end, it cost us nearly 500

fucking thousand dollars to make that album, and it was the biggest pile of horseshit that I've ever made in my life. I'm embarrassed by it."

The self-produced *Never Say Die!*, released in October 1978, was, indeed, woeful, although it reached number 12 in the UK and number 69 in America. Dressed with harmonica, brass and Don Airey's keyboards, it was overtly experimental but at the same time, very ordinary. Its only concessions to rock involved an unconvincing return to the bluesy jamming of their earliest days.

The experience of making the album told Ozzy that his big mistake had not been to leave Black Sabbath but to rejoin them. None of the four members were getting along well, Ozzy strongly disliked a couple of the road crew, and the relationship between him and Iommi had disintegrated to the point of no return.

A mellower Iommi now says: "When you were younger, things seemed to be more important. It wasn't as bad as it was made out to be; it was mainly that somebody had to be in charge of the band, and it was me that had to do all the saying, 'This is what we're going to do', or 'Let's do this.' If I didn't, then we'd all be looking at each other with our fingers up our arse."

Ozzy said: "It was a real bad mess – Black Sabbath was as black as its name at the end of the day." He added: "We were all totally fucked up on drugs and alcohol, in a terrible state with cocaine and booze and fucking uppers and downers and pot and this and that, and we just forgot how to do it together."

They forgot how to do *everything* together, by all accounts. Lambasting Iommi, Butler and Ward as "boring old farts", Ozzy complained: "There I was, this crazy guy, still into wrecking hotel rooms and having parties. It just didn't work. I mean, how can you go up onstage and shout, 'Yeah, I love you all! Rock'n'roll forever!' and then go to bed at 10 o'clock with a nightcap on, a candle in your hand and a Bible under your arm? But that was what the others were into."

There were other problems, too: "Whatever I suggested, the band didn't like. No one listened to me at all... you've got no idea how that feels." The family atmosphere that Ozzy had so missed during his three months away from the band had simply vanished.

Said Ozzy: "In the early days it was all for one and one for all. In the end it was everybody for themselves. It got bitchy and catty." And then there was the music: "The last two or three albums with Sabbath I didn't enjoy. The last one I hated."

This state of affairs limped along until 1979 when the band had finished a tour, with Van Halen opening, and returned to Los Angeles. There, Ozzy allegedly showed little inclination to rehearse, and the rest of the band decided that he had to go. Close friend Bill Ward volunteered to break the news.

"Ozzy was in really bad shape at that time," said Bill. "We were not accomplishing a whole lot... I reluctantly pitched in and agreed that we would need another singer. In one sense, it was a very proper decision, but in another sense it is incredibly sad. It was the right thing to approach him directly and talk to him.

"After I got sober, I realized that I lied to Tony, Geezer, Ozzy and myself. I didn't want to be in a band without Ozzy."

Talking of the "monstrosity" that Sabbath became, Ozzy said: "Tony and I didn't talk any more. It was all a bit sad, and a really depressing end to the band."

But looking back: "We had some good laughs, sure, especially with Bill. He was always good for a crack,

but Geezer was forever moaning about how he wanted to take a year's holiday. And Tony was kind of difficult to get on with. He used to be quiet for hours and then he'd suddenly do something mad, which he thought was funny. I mean, once he set fire to Bill's beard, which was really dangerous. But Bill was great... he just breathed in this big cloud of fumes and said, 'Hmm – a good smoke, that.'"

Iommi has uproarious memories of Ozzy, too. "We were all in an elevator in this real plush hotel, and Ozzy decides to take a crap. As he's doing it, the elevator is going down to the reception floor. The door suddenly opens, and there's Ozzy with his pants around his knees. And all these people in fur coats are just staring at him with their mouths open..."

Such shameless exploits contributed to Ozzy's "wildman of rock" reputation, although his outrages would become more sensational as time went on.

As a member of Black Sabbath, however, he earned genuine respect from millions. "It's only after I left Sabbath that I realized how great an influence it was."

Never Say Die!

The title came from Bill Ward. He'd been searching his imagination for a theme which would be strong and mobilizing, something to motivate and steer the band through their miserable recording sessions in Canada.

"Never Say Die!" occurred to him as his head teemed with images of Britishness – the RAF, and the national attitude. "Chin up, chaps!" – Ozzy liked that.

"Oh don't you ever, don't ever say die/Never, never, never say die again" urge the lyrics, which towards the end return to the theme of children as the potential saviours of civilization. The song itself verges on power-chord pop, and it's one of those most often cited in defence of the album by loyal Sabbath fans who have pointed to its bright pace, passable riff and up-front, untreated vocals as evidence that the old dog was not dead.

In general, the album production – credited to the band – has been widely criticized for its layered approach, its multi-tracking, reverb and other studio tricks, a debilitating mix which often submerged the vocals, and a poor sound quality.

Ozzy concurred: "I wasn't really happy with the way things were going over the last two or three albums before I left. I mean, it was really getting away from everything Sabbath had been based on in the first place. What we needed was a good, strong producer who

could direct us in the studio and someone who wasn't too directly involved in the band personally. Instead, we were producing ourselves and getting lost."

He added: "We couldn't reproduce what we were doing in the studio, cos it was so overdubbed with 300 voices and all that. Tony would do seven guitar overdubs and I felt like I had to compete in a way to stay part of it... it was so bizarre... multi-tracking voices and backward harmonies... drowning people's brains with all this scientific bullshit I don't understand."

Released as a single and a taster for the album in the summer of 1978, "Never Say Die!" enjoyed a number 21 chart slot in the UK and earned Black Sabbath an appearance on "Top Of the Pops".

JUNIOR'S EYES

Ozzy rewrote the lyrics to say goodbye to his father, Jack. In its original form, this was one of the Dave Ward collaborations, and it changed little musically in the crossover. A dreary mid-tempo number, it outstays its welcome as it ploughs towards the seven-minute mark in a welter of improvisation.

However, the hugely personal sentiments expressed by Ozzy endow the song with a validity it would not otherwise have deserved.

"Junior's eyes, they couldn't disguise the pain/His father was leaving and Junior's grieving again," sings a devastated son.

Ozzy has described in painful detail the heartbreak of his cancer-stricken father's last days and funeral. He told one interviewer: "They put him in a fucking closet with the fucking mops and buckets because he was on the death ward and it was too distressing for the rest of the patients. So they put him in a cot, sort of a crib thing, a giant crib.

"They strapped him like a boxer, fucking bandages on his hands, with a glucose drip going into his arm. He was stoned out of his head...

"I told my father one day, 'I take drugs. Before you go, will you take drugs?' He says, 'I promise you I'll take drugs.'

"He was totally out of his mind on morphine, because the pain must have been horrendous. They had the operation on a Tuesday and he died on Thursday. No one could understand what he was talking about, because he was so out of it. He says to me – he only understands drugs as 'speed' – he says, 'Ssspeeeed.' And he died in my arms."

Ozzy continued: "When they go, they're out of their misery. What freaked me out more than anything else was the funeral. I was singing fucking 'Paranoid' in the church... on Seconal [a sedative], drunk... it blew me

away. All the family came that I'd never seen for fucking years, and they were making comments. In England, it's a weird scene at a fucking death. My father hated his brother Harold – my whole family's fucking nuts."

AIR DANCE

The most contentious track on the album, "Air Dance" is loved and loathed in equal measure by the Sabbath following. Those who enjoy it do so perversely, since it sounds absolutely alien, quite unlike anything the band had ever attempted. For the same reasons, it's despised by hardliners, appalled that Sabbath could even contemplate such a betrayal.

The lyrics describe a stereotypical, nostalgic scene in which an elderly lady, surrounded by fading photographs, looks back on her lost youth as a beautiful, carefree dancer. "The days grow lonely for the dancing queen/And now she dances only in her dreams," laments Ozzy.

The song's great crime was to introduce a certain jazz element, creating an atmosphere for the laid-back piano, the brass and Iommi's lead guitar excursions. Ozzy had strong feelings about the jazz inclinations of Iommi and Ward especially: "Onstage, Tony used to go into these great long guitar solos which were like jazz. I mean, jazz at a Black Sabbath gig – ridiculous. I used to watch him from the side of the stage and cringe when Tony did that sort of thing. I used to hide. I'm not knocking him technically because I still think he's a really brilliant guitar player. But his jazz solos used to slow things down."

BREAKOUT

A brass-led instrumental, "Breakout" drove another long thorn into Ozzy's flesh. It enjoys the distinction of being described by one reviewer as "the worst Iommi has written in a long line of space-filling instrumentals".

Ozzy complained: "On the last album, on that track 'Breakout', I couldn't believe it one Sunday morning when 30 guys with trumpets marched in and started playing on a Black Sabbath album. It nearly made my hair fall out."

He went further: "Tony was always trying to make the band more sophisticated. I mean, there was one time when he brought in a load of string players on a session. I walked into the studio and there were all these guys of about 50 sitting around waiting for their go. I thought to myself, 'What the hell is all this?' I mean, violinists on a Black Sabbath album! If I'd been a fan, I wouldn't have believed it."

Ozzy admitted: "I wanted to get back to good, basic, hard rock like we were known for. I wouldn't have minded doing the new stuff if it was reproduceable onstage, but it wasn't. Fucking hell, it took so long to do. It was done in three sections and joined together. No way could you do that onstage – they'd think you were R2D2. Studios drive me up the wall. After a month or two in one of those places, I feel like a bat.

"Fuck this overdubbing and all that mechanical crap, Tony Iommi playing through a jar of Vaseline or something."

"Showing up on those later albums was just each individual going a little bit more in their own direction," reasoned Bill Ward. "There were more differences going on as we were all growing... Each of us is very talented and can do a lot of things other than the phenomenon that is Black Sabbath – I see that as the four of us. We are capable of so much more as individual people. Ozzy is a great example of that."

Other tracks on *Never Say Die!* are the keyboard-heavy riff-rocker "Johnny Blade" – a portrait of the meanest guy in town – with a two-minute guitar solo beloved of some fans; the plodding, jamming "A Hard Road", which tritely talks of the harshness of life but hopes for a better future and features backing vocals from Butler and Iommi (in the only singing he ever did for Black Sabbath); "Shock Wave", whose black moon, blood red sky, blood brew, wind of mist, ghostly shadows, evil power and crawling body receive scant musical justice in this standard rock riff-and-solo work-out; "Over To You", a prog-orientated protest at the state's brainwashing of schoolchildren; and "Swinging The Chain", rock'n'rolling with a Bill Ward vocal that leaps from softly-softly familiarity into a series of primal screams as he plunders his military fixations from the viewpoint of World War II.

Tracks on the preceding album, *Technical Ecstasy*, are: "Back Street Kids", "You Won't Change Me", "It's Alright", "Gypsy", "All Moving Parts (Stand Still)", 'Rock'n'Roll Doctor", "She's Gone" and "Dirty Women".

"Goodnight... and goodbye!"

Blizzard of Ozz

"The first song I ever learned was "Crazy Train"
by Ozzy Osbourne. The opening riff is the perfect
guitar riff... My friend inspired me
to buy a guitar, but hearing Randy Rhoads
for the first time made me want to learn how to play it."
GREG TRIBBETT (AKA GURGG), MUDVAYNE

Ozzy relives his last days in Sabbath

Something is missing.

Ozzy with the spectacular Randy Rhoads

Black Sabbath went back to work with Ronnie James Dio – the first in a succession of vocalists – while Ozzy sat in a room in LA's Le Parc Hotel and broke his heart.

He stayed there for more than three months with the curtains closed, surrounded by overflowing ashtrays and all the debris of a life spent indoors, only picking up the phone to send out for pizza, liquor and cocaine. "I was suicidal," he later admitted. Haunted by insecurity and a dread of ending up back at the abattoir, he degenerated into "a fucking fat, stupid mess... fat and stupid and drugged."

As legend has it, Sharon Arden magically came back into his life with some surprising news: her father Don Arden's management company had decided to drop Black Sabbath and take on Ozzy Osbourne as a solo artist. Also on offer was a deal with Arden's Jet Records.

"I was amazed," said Ozzy. "Sharon and me had nothing going at the time – in actual fact, she was seeing Tony Iommi – but there she was."

As rumours abounded throughout the rest of 1979 that Ozzy intended to call his new band Son Of Sabbath, he returned to England to put together a group called Blizzard Of Ozz. Their eponymously titled first album would rehabilitate Ozzy as a major force in heavy metal. It would also introduce a new guitar hero – the diminutive but legendary Randy Rhoads.

The first recruit was bass player and lyricist Bob Daisley, an ex-Rainbow man.

He told interviewer Jeb Wright: "People told me that I was making a mistake... that Ozzy was a burnt-out has-been and that he was a pisshead. I just had a good feeling about the whole thing. I said, 'Fuck, I'm going to do it.' It was the sort of work that I had been looking for, you know, heavy rock.

"Ozzy did do a bit of coke and he smoked a bit of pot, but I think he drank more than anything. I used to get on his case and I think he got pissed off about it... I used to jog in those days to stay fit, and I would take Ozzy with me to get him away from the shit and to give him more of a healthy feeling."

Somewhere along the line in LA, Ozzy had bumped into Randy Rhoads – a young guitarist from Santa Monica with a band called Quiet Riot. Randy was flown to London and, from there, he travelled with Daisley to the Midlands town of Stafford, where Ozzy was living.

"I'm as happy as a pig in shit at the moment. Couldn't be happier. I don't really think about Sabbath any more... I don't care what they do."

Ozzy said: "When he turned up, unfortunately, I was stoned out of my mind. I mean, I was on another planet. Some guy woke me up and said, 'He's here.' I looked up and Randy started playing from this tiny amp. Even in my semi-consciousness, he blew my mind. I told him to come by the next day and that he had the gig." Finding a drummer proved more difficult. Lee Kerslake, formerly of Uriah Heep – the last to be auditioned – fitted in perfectly and the jigsaw was complete, with keyboardist Don Airey recruited for the sessions.

With most of the songs already written, the band retired to a residential studio in Monmouthshire, Wales, to complete the material with the intention that the album, which they would produce themselves, would be be hard, heavy and straightforward.

Asked about Ozzy's attitude in the studio, Daisley told Jeb Wright that the singer was not a perfectionist: "He is to a point, but I would get very serious about the music and the production and about rehearsing and getting parts right. He used to jokingly call me Sid Serious: "Fucking come on, Sid Serious, lighten up.'"

"I am easy-going in the studio, and I like to have a laugh as much as anyone else, but I take my music serious. Randy did as well... Randy was really just

starting to come alive in his playing. All due respect to Randy, he was a brilliant player, a great player and a dedicated player, but I think the chemistry between the four people brought out the best in everybody, including Randy and Ozzy."

Ozzy gives greater credit to Rhoads, describing him as "phenomenal" and remembering: "Randy was the first guy that ever gave me time. I have a lot of ideas in my head, but being as how I don't play an instrument, to put them across musically is very difficult for me. Randy had the patience and the time to hear me out and work ideas out with me..."

Ozzy also enthused: "When we were recording, he would disappear in the studio for days. I'd ask him what he was doing and he would say, 'I'm working on this solo and I still can't get it.' Finally, it would come to him and he would call me and say, 'Listen to this.' It would always tear my head off."

Randy Rhoads' innovative and emotional guitar work on the two albums he completed with Ozzy before he was killed in a plane crash is revered to this day.

Blizzard Of Ozz – with all songs credited to Osbourne, Rhoads and Daisley – was released in the UK by Jet in September 1980 and in the US six months later by Jet-CBS. It reached numbers seven and 21 respectively, and quickly achieved quadruple-platinum sales.

It was a landmark album for Ozzy and for the rock scene, which responded to the fresh and compelling vigour of this combination of bad-assed musical poke, darkly troubled lyrics, tension, dynamics, up-tempos and broad likeability. Add to this Rhoads' guitar virtuosity, fleshing out the brain-mashing riffs of Ozzy's past with dazzling fills and runs, and the odd psuedo-classical adventure, and the album was a winner.

"I'm as happy as a pig in shit at the moment," beamed Ozzy. "Couldn't be happier. I don't really think about Sabbath any more... I don't care what they do."

Late, lamented and legendary

The small but perfectly talented Randy

CRAZY TRAIN

Ozzy wrote some sleeve notes for his future compilation album *The Ozzman Cometh*. He explained that "Crazy Train" – "I'm going off the rails on a crazy train!" – was about "everything I was going through at the time" and traced the song's origins to the studio in Wales.

"The studio was rumoured to be haunted by a poltergeist," he wrote. "Most days we would wake up and windows would be smashed, crockery shattered, doors were broken off their hinges and our clothes would be floating in the stream outside. The studio owner was insisting that it was us getting drunk every night and tearing up the studio, but we stuck by our story that it was always the poltergeist."

"'Crazy Train' is really a peace song about how crazy it is that people are brainwashed and mind-controlled by the powers-that-be over fucking stupid religion and stuff like that," added Bob Daisley, talking to Jeb Wright. "That is why the opening lines are, 'Crazy but that's how it goes/Millions of people living as foes'. We have inherited all the bullshit from all of the cold wars and all of the crap. The young people inherited it, and back then *I* was still young."

While many fans assume that Ozzy wrote his own lyrics, Daisley retorted that he, in fact, supplied all of them for *Blizzard Of Ozz* and the following albums *Diary Of A Madman*, *Bark At The Moon*, *The Ultimate Sin* and *No Rest For The Wicked*.

Often, they were purpose-built for Ozzy to sing. Daisley said: "We started putting music together – just me and Randy and Ozzy. Ozzy had these vocal melodies and he would sing them with any words that came into his head. Ozzy and Randy sat up one night trying to

write lyrics and I came down and saw what they had done... I told them, 'I tell you what, I will write the lyrics.'

"What I am most proud of is 'Crazy Train'. Randy came up with the riff and Ozzy came up with the vocal melody and I wrote the lyrics and the musical section that Randy soloed over in the middle. It has become a rock'n'roll anthem, and I am really proud of that."

"Crazy Train" finds Ozzy's vocals and Rhoads' flashing guitar locked tight into a hard-rock groove that appealed well beyond the metal community.

Rhoads was not just fire and thunder

Goodbye to Romance

The slow and strongly melodic "Goodbye To Romance" stands as Ozzy's farewell to Black Sabbath and his commitment to the future. Laced with Rhoads' sympathetic and moving guitar work, it's all the more poignant for the fact that at the time he recorded it, Ozzy had no idea how promising his future really was. It's said that when he played his first concert with Blizzard Of Ozz in autumn 1980 in Scotland – the band appearing, informally, for a couple of gigs under the name of Law, prior to the tour proper – he burst into tears at the tumultuous audience reaction: it was the moment he realized he could make it on his own.

"I've been the king, I've been the clown/Still broken wings can't hold me down – I'm free again," sang Ozzy. If Daisley did indeed write the lyrics, he couldn't have tailored them better to the situation of his vocalist. The song ends on a positive note with the sun coming out to banish any lingering shadows of the past.

Suicide Solution

With "Suicide Solution", Ozzy's past comes back to haunt him with a vengeance.

A trudging metal classic fronted by the ranting Ozzy, it was seriously misinterpreted by certain individuals who continued to associate the singer with a demonic underworld, people who only zoomed in on the title and clearly didn't look too hard at the lyrics, which plainly warn of the perils of alcohol abuse.

This had tragic consequences: a teenager killed himself in America, and his parents thereafter sued Ozzy, alleging that their son had acted after hearing "Suicide Solution". This was not the last time Ozzy would be dragged through the courts by parents blaming him for their children's deaths.

The case was dismissed, and Ozzy said: "This kid who committed suicide – it was never my intention to write a song so a kid would put a fucking gun to his head. I copped the fucking blame." He also looked at the wider dangers: "America is getting heavy. Anything sensational, they just go for it. I'm desperately frightened that some guy's going to blow me away. Some of these guys are nuts. They want to take it too far. All it is, you know, I'm a clown. A terrible old showbiz ham... So why do they take it all so seriously?"

"Wine is fine but whiskey's quicker/Suicide is slow with liquor," states the song unequivocally, using the word "solution" to mean "liquid" and not "answer".

Referring to the death of AC/DC singer Bon Scott, Ozzy said: "He choked on his own vomit, and I was into the same sort of thing for a while, drinking to excess. That song is a warning. I don't want it to happen to me."

Many fans have since come to accept that the song is about Bon Scott (pictured). Bob Daisley: "'Suicide Solution' is about Ozzy, because he was drinking himself into an early grave... I knew Bon Scott and so did Ozzy, and we did find out about Bon Scott's death during the recording of that album. But I wrote the fucking words, so he (Ozzy) can say all he likes about who I wrote it about, but I wrote it about him killing himself with alcohol. It was a warning song. It's stupid to drink yourself into the ground. It is not a solution to a problem, as it is really just hiding."

No one can accuse Ozzy Osbourne of hiding from the reality of his drinking, although he frequently professed to be on the wagon – falling off again five minutes later.

"I have this little demon that keeps making me drink," he admitted in that same year. "I just love drinking and getting drunk. I'll drink anything. If it takes my fancy, I'll drink it. I'm the Dean Martin of heavy metal, I am. I'm not as mad as everyone makes out. I'm worse. I go mad on booze. I smash things up and set fire to myself. I set fire to my sleeve the other night when I fell in the fire, drunk.

"I drink Perrier water to cut my intake down. I don't want to be another rock'n'roll suicide. I laid off the booze totally for three or four weeks. I'd go into pubs surrounded by people full of beer and think, 'Was I as bad as that?' When I'm not at work, I get bored and start drinking."

MR CROWLEY

Ozzy rekindled his old Satanic connections with a song about the infamous black magician Aleister Crowley, although it isn't a particularly complimentary ode.

Opening with eerie organ music and with Ozzy's vocals sounding suitably haunting, the song rumbles solidly along as it accuses its subject: "You fooled all the people with magic/Yeah, you waited on Satan's call..."

"I'd read several books about Aleister Crowley," explained Ozzy. 'He was a very weird guy and I always wanted to write a song about him. While we were recording the *Blizzard Of Ozz* album, there was a pack of Tarot cards he had designed lying around the studio. Well, one thing led to another and the song 'Mr Crowley' was born."

Bob Daisley is happy to credit Ozzy with the idea and the title for the song. However, he has admitted to a guilty secret about the organ intro. "One of the auditions we had was a keyboard player who had an idea that went something like that. We got that idea and wrote that part for the beginning of 'Mr Crowley'." But no chance of a lawsuit: "I think we changed it enough!"

Blowing any last shred of Satanic majesty that may have been clinging to Ozzy, Daisley recalled: "One night (on the first tour), there was a big line of kids who wanted to get their albums signed after one of our gigs. One kid, as he got his Black Sabbath album signed, said, 'Ozzy, are you still into black magic?' Ozzy looked at him and said, 'No, I like Milk Tray now...'"

Other tracks on *Blizzard Of Ozz* include the perennial metallic favourite "I Don't Know", Ozzy's regular reply to fans expecting him to hold the secrets of life and, especially, death; the short and tender classical guitar instrumental "Dee", created by Rhoads for his mother; the fast but filler-standard "No Bone Movies" about a porn fan; the environmentally worried "Mother Earth", which was inspired by John Lennon's "Mother" and rises from slow beginnings through a synthesizer passage to a Rhoads guitar showcase; and "Steal Away (The Night)", a heavy rocker that's distinguished only by some sterling guitar work.

Diary of a Madman

"I knew something was going on with that music, and I had to get my hands on it. I immediately thought Ozzy ruled."

JOEY JORDISON,
SLIPKNOT,
ON THE BAT-BITING SCANDAL.

The events surrounding *Diary Of A Madman* would conspire to overshadow what was a significant release for Ozzy Osbourne. The drink- and drug-induced madness that he carried around like a timebomb finally exploded in a series of outrageous escapades that would dramatically heighten and define his notoriety.

Diary Of A Madman was a companion-piece to *Blizzard Of Ozz*. Recorded hard on the heels of that debut, it consolidated Ozzy's newly won credibility as a solo performer, a leader, fearlessly beating a path into the Eighties with a vital and exciting vision of heavy metal.

Crucially, it was the second and last studio album to enjoy the work of Ozzy's guitar whizzkid, co-writer and right-hand man, Randy Rhoads, whose death would bring this period of chaos to a tragic conclusion.

Perhaps a little heavier than its predecessor and arguably more rushed, *Diary Of A Madman* is hard-hitting, often complicated, sometimes gentle and usually melodic, and Rhoads' trademark playing remains inspirational. Released in October 1981, it reached number 14 in the UK and number 16 in the US.

At the same time, Bob Daisley and Lee Kerslake were given their marching orders. Daisley maintains that this was simply a ploy to bring in ex-Black Oak Arkansas drummer Tommy Aldridge, who had been busy with Pat Travers when Ozzy first formed the band. Daisley was replaced by Quiet Riot's Rudy Sarzo.

Daisley would later return to the Ozzy fold, playing on, and writing for, a string of subsequent albums. But in spite of this, he and Kerslake would go on to sue Ozzy, Sharon and all the connected companies, returning to the courts in 2000 to demand $20 million (£13 million) in the ongoing dispute over songwriting credits and payments, and use of material.

Ozzy's response was to remove their parts from *Blizzard Of Ozz* and *Diary Of A Madman* and to have them re-recorded by different musicians for the 2002 reissues – an action slammed by fans and critics alike who have accused him of tampering with history and of insulting Rhoads' memory.

Shortly after the pair's departure, Ozzy and Sharon Arden attended a marketing meeting with executives at CBS/Epic Records' offices in LA. Eager to protest at the coldness and hypocrisy of major record companies – and, more particularly, at what he saw as Epic's lack of effort on his behalf as an associated Jet artist – a drunken Ozzy entered the conference room with two allegedly live doves, one in each pocket, and, to everyone's horror, bit the head off one bird in a flurry of feathers and spurting blood.

"Be afraid. Be very afraid...

... I know where your cats live..."

Ozzy has since contended that he only intended to release the doves, but on discovering that one had died, simply went for the jugular "rather than waste it".

He was asked to leave the building. "You should have seen their faces," said Ozzy, afterwards. "They all went white. They were speechless…" And as for the dove: "It tasted warm, like tomato sauce," or, "like a good hamburger."

One staffer who witnessed the event is "99.9 per cent sure the dove was alive." She said, "I was in shock... it was horrible. Personally, I thought it was an awful thing to do, even if it was a fake bird."

News of the atrocity swept America, ensuring that Ozzy's *Diary Of A Madman* tour would be picketed by animal rights campaigners – and would also be turned into a gorefest like no other through his own, and the fans', unique efforts.

The huge, foggy castle forming the stage set was the least spectacular feature of the show. More interesting was the tour dwarf (apparently the actor who played R2D2 in *Star Wars*) who was nightly pelted with pig entrails, jammed into a hole and then hanged (safely

supported by a harness, it must be explained).

Never one to leave his audiences out of things, Ozzy threw 25lb (11kg) of offal into the crowd during each performance. Word travelled fast, and the fans began bringing along their own raw meat to participate in an exceptionally bloody food fight.

"It was insane, fucking hell, man, insane," exclaimed Ozzy later. "I was getting fucking chicken legs, fucking dead cats...

"One night a cop came backstage and says to me, 'Do you realize the effect you're having on these kids?' I said, 'It's just a bit of fun, what's the matter with you?' He showed me a photo of a kid waiting outside to go into the concert with a cow's head on his shoulder!"

In Ozzy's retellings of this story, the cow sometimes becomes a horse or an ox. And he has confided, and just as often denied, that he shot and stabbed with a sword the many cats he kept at home with first wife, Thelma. "The nice lady from next door peered over the fence and said, 'Ah, John, I see you're back. Unwinding.'"

Master of the anecdote and the outrageous punchline, Ozzy was an image-builder par excellence. But it's

Ozzy: "I am not fucking Dracula"

incontestable that he did, indeed, bite the head off a live bat. This was when the tour rolled into Des Moines in the New Year of 1982.

"I thought it was a plastic toy," said Ozzy, recalling the hail of inanimate objects that would usually assail him onstage. "So I just grabbed this thing, bit the head off and thought, 'Fuck me! It was flapping.'"

Later remembering his unusual snack as "not very nice – all crunchy and warm", he added: "It took a lot of water to down just that fucking bat's head, let me tell you. It's still stuck in my fucking throat, after all these years. People all over the world say, 'You're the guy who kills creatures? You still do it? You do it every night?' It happened fucking once, for Christ's sake." Even more unpalatable than the bat's head was the course of painful anti-rabies injections that the singer then had to undergo.

Slipknot's Joey Jordison was just one of the little kids growing up then in Des Moines who were simply transfixed by the episode.

Another day, another drama, and Ozzy has been typically inconsistent in his memories of his next great public offence, in February 1982. Arriving in San Antonio, Texas, he did, definitely, urinate all over the Alamo – a sacred monument to the 180-strong band of local people who died defending their state against an invading Mexican army.

Ozzy has sometimes denied the indiscretion, claiming that he was "pissed" and not "pissing", or has suggested that it was "a genuine mistake". But in his more candid moments, he has held his hands up, adding to the legend with this: "I can honestly say, all the bad things that ever happened to me were directly attributed to drugs and alcohol. I mean, I would never urinate at the Alamo at nine o'clock in the morning dressed in a woman's evening dress, sober."

There was no evening dress, and no early morning. Allan Jones, editor of *Uncut* magazine, was with Ozzy when it happened. He has confirmed: "Ozzy wasn't wearing a dress. He was wearing his wardrobe mistress' culottes and a straw Stetson. It must have been mid-to-late afternoon when we got down to the Alamo. We were pretty drunk by then, it must be said."

In his first-hand report recently reprinted by *Uncut*, Jones recalled the photo session at the famous landmark: "Ozzy's pulled down his culottes and is currently pissing quite torrentially all over the front of the shrine of Texas liberty."

Ozzy was whisked away by insulted police officers, locked up and arrested for public intoxication, for which he was fined something close to $200 (£130).

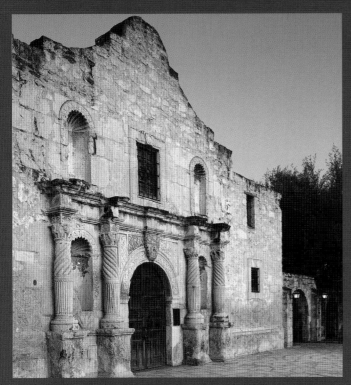

The Alamo: Texan shrine desecrated by Ozzy

"If my ideas seem disordered in intellect or slightly psychotic... it is because they are. I am Ozzy Osbourne."

The next month, however, would bring an end to all the shenanigans. On March 19, 1982, Randy Rhoads was killed after going for a spin in a small, private aircraft piloted by the driver of the group's tour bus.

OVER THE MOUNTAIN

Lee Kerslake opens the track, and the album, with a pounding drum pattern that has since become an essential trick of the metal trade.

A fast-paced and vigorous introduction, "Over The Mountain" was a radio hit that showcases Rhoads' individuality as a guitarist, mixing unorthodox scales, sounds and turns of phrase into the classic traditions of hard-riffing and soloing, and making it all sound like the most natural thing in the world. As one reviewer noted, "He could actually make a song live, breathe and still sound great two decades after it was recorded."

"The first LP was good, but too much of it was a reflection of what was going through my head about Sabbath," declared Ozzy. "This is much more like what I sound like – and when I record with the new band, well, there'll be no comparison."

Sadly, the new band would not include his best friend Rhoads, and the pair's unique chemistry died with this album.

Just after its release, Ozzy revealed that *Diary Of A Madman* had been "an idea of mine for the last five years".

He continued: "I am happy with the success of my debut *Blizzard Of Ozz* album and the tens of thousands of followers that have come out to see the shows, but I think something has changed me. I keep seeing visions of my birth, my life and my death. I have become infatuated with the feeling of horror.

"My fascination with life's phobias have manifested themselves on this new record. I only hope its tracks will freeze the blood and make the flesh creep to make people understand that this is Ozzy music. If my ideas seem disordered in intellect or slightly psychotic... it is because they are. I am Ozzy Osbourne."

Lyrically, "Over the Mountain" falls slightly short of blood-freezing, although its mystical travels through "life's magic astral plane" do alight on a certain, unhappy place: "Living in a daydream – only place I had to stay/Fever of a breakout burning in me

miles wide..." Still, the message is positive: unlock your own magic and fly!

FLYING HIGH AGAIN

"I can see through mountains – watch me disappear/I can even touch the sky…"

A feelgood pop-rocker, this is usually filed alongside an unapologetic Ozzy's other drug eulogies such as "Sweet Leaf" and "Snowblind".

Several years later, Ozzy compared these songs with the later, more cautionary tales in his repertoire. He said in 1985, "I suddenly realized that when I was a drug addict, I used to write things like 'Flying High Again', all this shit. And the other night, I thought, 'Fucking hell, I sing one song for it and then straight after, I sing

One... two... testing... riiiip!

one song against it.' But the thing is, that's OK. Because that was where I was when I wrote that, so why shouldn't I do it? It's part of my life. It's part of what I am and what I will be.

"I might start singing fucking religious songs. I don't think so, but if I choose to, why not? To think you can't sing stuff from your last album because now you're a different man is bullshit. If they're good to write and good enough to hear and to buy, then they're good enough to sing onstage, you know? I'm not ashamed of anything I've done in the past."

Bob Daisley recalls the writing sessions for the album: "We just worked five days a week, all day. Randy had riffs that he was working on... it was Lee, Randy and myself. A lot of times Ozzy wasn't there, as he either had hangovers or he was off to see his family.

"I know Lee came up with the vocal melody for 'Flying High Again'. He used to have a microphone at the side of his drums and he would sing while we put the songs together."

Daisley also told Jeb Wright a story about his teenage years in Sydney, Australia, where he played in a band: "We went to the country to do a gig. This was in the Sixties, and we were all dressed in our flower-power gear. We had on fringed jackets, flowery shirts and little square glasses. We must have looked really freaky to the country people.

"I had a station wagon and as I was loading my gear

after the gig, this country-looking guy came up to me and said, 'Are you going back down to the smoke tonight?' I said, 'Yeah.' To him, people in the city must have been weird and all on drugs, because he said, 'Are you going to be flying high again in Sydney town?'

"When I was writing the lyrics for 'Flying High Again' I was doing a bit of coke with Ozzy and I thought, 'Here I am flying high again,' and that guy's voice came back to me and I thought, 'Fuck, that is a good title.'"

YOU CAN'T KILL ROCK'N'ROLL

Ozzy's contempt for the record industry at this time was all-consuming. It gave rise to the notorious incident in which he bit the head off a dove, and it created the acid sentiments of "You Can't Kill Rock'n'Roll".

"Ozzy had the basic idea and I wrote all the lyrics for it," said Bob Daisley. "It is just about record companies being fucking greedy and trying to tell the artist what to do. They will tell you one thing and then do something else. It was really about record companies controlling, and the industry in general."

"Rock'n'roll is my religion and my law!" cries Ozzy, flying the flag in the face of the dirty, rotten, cheating bastards he saw all around him.

"How many times can they fill me with lies and I listen, again/Twisting the truth and they're playing around with my head – OK."

You can hear the passion in his vocals as the song, slow and filled with contrasting displays of brute force and gentleness, moves through its intricate arrangements. It's one of those that could have benefited from some judicious editing: many fans say they would have been willing to sacrifice a couple of minutes here and there across the album for the pleasure of an extra track.

S.A.T.O.

The initials represent Sharon Arden, Thelma Osbourne – or so one theory goes. Certainly, the lyrics would fit. As Ozzy himself would undoubtedly agree, you should never let the truth get in the way of a good story. So we'll discount, perhaps, the other likely explanation, that the abbreviation stands for Sailing Across The Ocean.

Sharon Arden had become much more involved with the band managerially during the writing sessions for *Diary Of A Madman*, and she was particularly close to Ozzy.

He said: "She was the first person in my life who had ever given me any encouragement because in Sabbath I

was the least meaningful member of the band. But Sharon came along, showed me respect and gave me encouragement – she educated me in my cleanliness and my mannerisms and my attitude and everything. She made me grow up and I just fell in love with her because she's great. And she sorted out all the business because, with business, I like to do as little as possible."

Ozzy had by now separated from Thelma, after years of forgetting where his front door was. According to one story, a drunken Ozzy rolled home one night to find his possessions outside the house. Warned that he would be

arrested if he set foot across the threshold, he walked away from the family home and from his marriage.

The scene was set for a formal relationship with Sharon. "I can't conceal it like I know I did before," sings Ozzy in a track which harks back, musically, to the earthy, rocking, bluesy heyday of Black Sabbath. "I got to tell you now/The ship is ready waiting on the shore." It is, moreover, a "ship of joy" which will "stop you failing".

Ozzy and Sharon were married on a beach in Maui, Hawaii, on July 4, 1982.

White wedding for the Prince Of Darkness

"Who the fuck do you think I am? Frank Zappa?"

DIARY OF A MADMAN

With Ozzy well on his way to becoming rock's most celebrated maniac, it was understandable that fans would look to these lyrics hoping for a glimpse into the tormented mind of the genius at work.

Ozzy doesn't disappoint, pouring out a disturbing picture of confusion, frustration and manic depression – "Voice in the darkness/Scream away my mental health," he urges, chillingly.

"I really wrote that one about myself," explained Bob Daisley, rather surprisingly. "When I was 16 I had my first nervous breakdown and it really fucked me up. I was a sensitive kid and I have always been a sensitive person. I suppose you have to be sensitive, being in the arts. I wrote the words about myself.

"Quite often we have problems and we are our own worst enemies, and that is why 'enemies fill up the pages', one by one in the diary. 'Are they me?' I am my own worst enemy."

Ozzy was reportedly bewildered at first by the musical construction. Said Daisley: "Randy had the rough idea for the song, and I came up with the title. One day Ozzy came in and we played him *Diary Of A Madman* and because it had funny timings, he couldn't get his head around it. He said, 'Who the fuck do you think I am? Frank Zappa?'

"We said, 'You sing in this part but you don't sing here. This timing goes like this,' etc. He started to like it when he got his head around it, but at first he was like, 'This is not for me.'"

It was the band's most challenging song to date, closing the album in epic style with its differing movements. Neo-classical guitar licks give way to a monstrous riff, quiet interludes erupt into violent rock explosions, and string sounds and choral chanting add to the general, unsettling air of unpredictability, underpinned by a wicked bass.

At the time, there were plans for a film of the same name. "It'll be like an underground movie, a lot like the truth," enthused Ozzy. "Not all the phoney, glamour side of rock. I hate all that posing.

"Why can't people just be people and throw up now and again? We all crap, even the Queen..."

It would've been some movie. Many years later, it turned into some soap opera...

Other tracks on the album are "Believer", whose heavy, bass-driven menace is at odds with its positive advice about self-belief; "Little Dolls", the gruesomely detailed story of a voodoo victim (believed by some to be a metaphor for alcoholism) sung by Ozzy on both lead and harmony vocals, set to an ordinary hard rock/bluesy soundtrack; and the forlorn and fairly average piano ballad "Tonight".

Bark at the Moon

"Ozzy is a nice enough person, certainly a wizard of maximum clever resource utility, but not the kinda guy I hang out with much. I need to communicate with my people, and I can't understand anything he says! But God bless him and his family."
TED NUGENT

Ozzy (centre) with (l-r): Tommy Aldridge, Jake E Lee, Bob Daisley and Don Airey

Rewinding: Randy Rhoads and Bob Daisley were standing on a railway platform in Stafford, waiting for a train to London after the tiny guitarist's successful audition for Ozzy Osbourne.

Suddenly, Daisley had the strangest feeling. "I thought, 'One day, people are going to ask me what it was like to play with Randy Rhoads.' I had no idea that the album (*Blizzard Of Ozz*) was going to take off like it did, or that he was going to die in a few years."

Fast-forwarding: In the spring of 1982, Ozzy and his band were travelling in their tour bus from Knoxville, Tennessee, to Orlando, Florida, for a concert with Foreigner and UFO. Crossing over into the sunshine state, they stopped off near a town called Leesburg where the bus company was based; their vehicle needed some repairs.

Ozzy and Sharon slept on when the bus drew to a

halt, but other members of the entourage decided to accept an invitation from driver Andrew Aycock to take a ride in his private plane, a Beechcraft Bonanza. Keyboard player Don Airey and tour manager Jake Duncan went first. Randy Rhoads and wardrobe mistress Rachael Youngblood stepped aboard for the second flight. Aycock suddenly started buzzing the tour bus, circling it three times before clipping it. The plane spun into a nearby house and exploded, killing all on board.

Drug tests later established that the pilot had taken cocaine, and there was speculation that he had started dive-bombing the tour bus because his ex-wife was standing outside it.

Kevin Dubrow from Rhoads' old band, Quite Riot, surmised: "If they were buzzing the bus like people say, it probably meant that Randy was struggling with the

pilot to stop him from crashing it."

Ozzy Osbourne stated in an affidavit: "At approximately 9am on Friday, March 19, 1982, I was awoken from my sleep by a loud explosion. I immediately thought we'd hit a vehicle on the road. I got out of bed screaming to my fiancée, Sharon: 'Get off the bus!' After getting out of the bus, I saw that a plane had crashed. I didn't know who was on the plane at the time. When we realized that our people were on the plane, I found it very difficult to get assistance from anyone to help. In fact, it took almost a half-hour before anyone arrived." It's been reported that Ozzy dragged a deaf man out of the inferno that had once been a house.

Hours later, Bob Daisley and Lee Kerslake, having heard the news, were "drunk and crying" at the bar of a club in Houston, Texas, "drinking all of the drinks that Randy used to drink, like a Grasshopper and all these sort of cocktail drinks".

Numb in the aftermath, Ozzy had to rethink his entire career. At first, he assumed it was over. He recalled: "In the few short years before Randy died, I had gone through so much. My father had died, I got kicked out of Sabbath – I was up and down, up and down. Then Randy got killed. At that point I said to Sharon, 'I can't keep doing this.'" Sharon's advice was to keep on going, because that's what Rhoads would've wanted.

"Randy was a truly wonderful guy, and I'm not just saying that because he's dead," said Ozzy in tribute. "I think, had he lived, he'd have blown the balls off Eddie Van Halen…"

He later stated: "The fondest memory of Randy Rhoads is just him. He was an incredible talent… He was a lot of fun. If ever I could say I was in love with another man, I was in love with his spirit. I mean, not in

a physical sense. But he was beyond a friend to me."

And, significantly: "Randy Rhoads will always remind me of a time in my life and career when things took off again."

Facing yet another new beginning without his friend and ace collaborator, Ozzy battled through a black depression to take Sharon's advice. He recruited guitarist Bernie Torme, temporarily, to help get the tour back on the road in April, with Night Ranger's Brad Gillis taking over for the concluding dates.

Ozzy also scrapped his existing plans for a live album featuring the Rhoads band. Instead, he released a double-set of Black Sabbath covers recorded at the Ritz Club in New York with the Brad Gillis line-up. *Talk Of The Devil*, called *Speak Of The Devil* in America, hit the stores in November 1982, charting at number 21 and number 14 in the UK and the US respectively.

Interestingly, Sabbath's own *Live Evil* album, released two months later, reported a number 13 chart placing in the UK and number 37 in the US.

Talk Of The Devil released Ozzy from his obligations to Jet Records. Now, in addition to a new label deal, he wanted to transfer his management to Sharon. Her father, Don Arden, was not too happy; he made things as difficult as possible for the couple, forcing them to buy the contract for a reputed $1.5 million (£1 million). Father and daughter only recently started talking again, after twenty years.

With Ozzy signed to CBS/Epic, It was time for another studio album and yet another cabinet reshuffle. Ex-Ratt guitarist Jake E Lee took over from Gillis. And Bob Daisley returned to the fold to succeed Don Costa. Costa had replaced former UFO man Pete Way, who'd stepped in after Rudy Sarzo returned to Quiet Riot.

Ozzy, Lee, Daisley and Tommy Aldridge together recorded *Bark At The Moon*. Released to rave reviews in December 1983, it scored substantially with chart positions of number 24 (UK) and number 19 (US).

In truth, it's a patchy album, but its emotional background is compelling; its inconsistency is both understandable and forgiveable. Ozzy has blamed the mixing process for the album's erratic results.

Brad Gillis: replaced by Jake E Lee

BARK AT THE MOON

"The title for this song actually came from a joke I used to tell, where the punchline was, 'Eat shit and bark at the moon'," said Ozzy. "I'd had the vocal line for this and Jake came up with the riff. It was the first song we wrote together."

Although Ozzy receives sole writing credit for the tracks on the album, they were conceived collaboratively, with Jake E Lee also contributing "Rock'n'Roll Rebel" and Daisley claiming responsibility for most if not all of the lyrics.

For a song which arose from a joke, "Bark At The Moon" – a rousing opener – is appropriately cartoonish, a Hammer Horror werewolf story related in ghoulish detail: "Howling in shadows, living in a lunar spell/He finds his heaven spewing from the mouth of hell…"

Entering into the spirit of things for the video, Ozzy acts out a werewolf fantasy with relish, to the great enjoyment of MTV viewers. All good, clean, trick-or-treat-style fun – or so one might imagine.

> ## "I can't even fart without someone saying it caused their cat to jump on a fire."

In Canada, however, a 20-year-old man "felt strange inside" when he heard it. He felt so "strange" that, finally, he stabbed to death a 44-year-old woman and her two sons.

James Jollimore, from Halifax, committed the murders on New Year's Eve 1983. One of his friends revealed in court: "Jimmy said that every time he listened to the song ("Bark At The Moon"), he felt strange inside. He said when he heard it on New Year's Eve, he went out and stabbed someone."

This is a cross that Ozzy has had to bear throughout his career. While distraught parents have accused him of encouraging their children to kill themselves or others, Ozzy has rather acted as a magnet for the sort of teenagers who were already likely to commit such acts.

As he said himself: "Parents have called me and said, 'When my son died of a drug overdose, your record was on the turntable.' I can't help that. These people are freaking out anyway, and they need a vehicle for the freak-outs."

"Suicide Solution" had triggered a spate of deaths. By the turn of the Nineties, Ozzy had been sued by three separate families, each alleging that the song was to blame for the suicide of their child.

The first was a 19-year-old Californian youth called John who shot himself in the head while listening to "Suicide Solution". When his body was found, he was reportedly still wearing his headphones. Eric, a 14-year old Minnesota fan of Ozzy and Sabbath, turned a gun on himself the day after allegedly holding a séance in which he tried to contact dead rock stars.

Ozzy was further accused of sneaking subliminal messages on to his albums and of introducing 'hemisync' tones, which are created by soundwaves and are said to influence the listener's responses.

An attorney called Thomas Anderson, representing the family of John, contended that "Suicide Solution" contained a subliminal message recorded at one and a half times the usual speed of speech – "Why try, why

try? Get the gun and try it! Shoot, shoot, shoot!" – and hemisync tones which made John susceptible to the "instruction".

Ozzy's defence retorted that this was bollocks and that, furthermore, Ozzy was entitled to write about whatever he wanted. The case went all the way to the appeals court, which upheld the decision in Ozzy's favour. The following lawsuits against Ozzy were also dismissed.

"I swear on my life I never said, 'Get the fucking gun'," insisted Ozzy. He also explained: "I can't take responsibility for it. Causing their deaths was not my intention. If they think so, then I feel sorry for them too. You've got to try and ignore it, because around each corner there lurks another writ…

"What makes it even more annoying is that it's often done with the ulterior motive, such as a husband who's running for President, and they want to get as much publicity for their campaign…

"What's the difference between records and horror films? It's all entertainment, yet film directors aren't held responsible for deaths like we are. It's just so annoying."

More recently, he declared: "I can't even fart without someone saying it caused their cat to jump on a fire. I did this controversial chat show in America and they were saying my music causes kids to fucking go Satanic and all this crap. In America, one of the craziest nights of the year is Halloween when they all dress up as fucking gooks and freaks and monsters and whatever. Yet, when I do it every night of the week onstage, they term me a fucking anti-Christ. Take that Madonna video with those burning crosses ("Like A Prayer") – I'd have my arse nailed to a fucking cross if I did that."

Now You See It (Now You Don't)
Another people-pleasing hard-rocker, "Now You See It (Now You Don't)" simply heaves with sexual allusions – "Can I ask a question, d'ya think that you can take a blow?/That is why I always come and go, yeah."

This is unusual for Ozzy, who was never the greatest champion of groupies and their services. He once memorably remarked: "People say, 'Brilliant! Chicks! All the dope! All the booze! You have parties every night!' But it gets boring. I got to the point where I said, 'Why am I doing this?' I'm screwing some groupie and I think, 'What fucking disease have I caught now?' You know, shitting myself, every two seconds looking at my dick seeing if it's still on me… it's absolutely not worth it for me. Half the time I wouldn't know whether I'd done it or not because I was so fucking out of it, and I'd get so guilty I'd get fucked up again."

More recently, he declared: "In the old days when I used to drink, I'd wake up in the morning thinking, 'I don't know my name, I don't know where *you're* from and I know I'm not the first guy you've done this week.' Then when AIDS started, I just thought, 'Forget it.' I was seeing guys coming out of the clap clinic thanking God that they'd only caught syphilis."

Centre of Eternity

Caught in some sort of black hole, Ozzy describes the place right in the middle of infinity where, "There's no present, there's no future, I don't even know about the past..." He marries this to a riotous up-tempo that finds Jake E Lee kicking hard into his new role in the band.

It was an unenviable task, stepping into the vacancy left by the adored Randy Rhoads, and when Lee received his first call about the job, he didn't want to know. Cautiously changing his mind, he tried out along with 24 other hopefuls, ended up on a shortlist of three and almost blew his chances by arriving 45 minutes late for the final audition.

He told writer Steven Rosen: "Some guy said Ozzy almost walked out the door. He said, 'Fuck it. If this guy doesn't care enough to show up on time and he's going to be this kind of problem, forget it. I don't care how good he is.'"

Lee had no idea how he'd be received as Randy's replacement. He said, "If somebody comes up to me and goes, 'Man, you're number one, you're the best guitar player in the world,' I start feeling stupid. I go, 'Nah, there are guys better than me.' But if somebody comes up and says, 'You really suck, you're nothing compared to Randy,' then I go, 'Hey, fuck you. I'm good. I'm probably ten times better than you'll ever be.'"

Bob Daisley said: "Nobody knew how Ozzy's career was going to go at that time, because Randy was dead. It was going to be a whole different ballgame. I think Jake E Lee did a good job of filling Randy's shoes. I thought he was a great player. Ozzy has had other players who were a bit of a copy of Randy, either image-wise or playing-wise, or 'I used to be a pupil of Randy' or whatever. Jake E had his own style and his own sound. He didn't play like Randy, although he did play the Randy stuff very well. He did an admirable job. And I think the album turned out very good."

So Tired

A big, orchestral ballad with piano and a lot of melody, this portrayal of lost love was treated to a video which Ozzy, for one, will remember for a long time.

In one scene, a mirror shatters as Ozzy stands in front of it, clenching his fists. But during filming, someone over-estimated the strength of the charge which was set off to shatter the mirror: the glass exploded into Ozzy's face.

The song, meanwhile, has divided critics and fans alike. One reviewer proposed that it was "maybe the best ballad of Ozzy's career", while another pronounced it "dismal".

Among its detractors is none other than Jake E Lee who confessed to Steven Rosen: "The strings on 'Bark At The Moon' I hated. 'So Tired' I hated."

Lee was not entirely comfortable with his place in the scheme of things. He said: "On *Bark At The Moon*, I approached it really cautiously, because I was the new guy and I could be out any second, so I just played him (Ozzy) riffs and if he liked the riff, then the whole band would work on it.

Ozzy bares his chest for the new guitarist, Jake E Lee

"I didn't argue too much if I didn't like the way something was coming out. I'd go, 'I don't really like this.' And they'd go, 'Well, what do *you* know?' And I'd go, 'I don't know anything…'

"I'd present something and they'd fight, debate, say it sucked or whatever. Everybody contributed a little bit, and it didn't necessarily come out the way I imagined it would."

In another interview, Lee complained that the band did not allow him time to experiment with different guitar sounds: "Once we all arrived at something, they said, 'Do all the songs with this tone.' Well, I like variety and I like to have the creative freedom to search for the right guitar, the right amp, the right sound for any particular solo or song."

Other songs on the album are the synth-based "You're No Different", a retort to critics; the raucous "Rock'n'Roll Rebel", reasserting Ozzy's outlaw stance; the self-explanatory "Slow Down" (on the US version only), an average rocker; "Waiting For Darkness" which is uneventful, despite its stabs at creative melody; and the UK track, "Spiders", especially for arachnophobics: "Creepy crawly things filling up your bed/Soon you'll feel him crawling through your brains…" In the end, of course, "The spider's really me…" and "There's no escaping the spiders in your head."

Tracks on the preceding *Talk Of The Devil* album are "Symptom Of The Universe", "Snowblind", "Black Sabbath", "Fairies Wear Boots", "War Pigs", "The Wizard", "N.I.B.", "Sweet Leaf", "Never Say Die!", "Sabbath Bloody Sabbath", "Iron Man – Children Of The Grave" and "Paranoid".

Ozzy and "the miserabilest man God ever bred": Jake E Lee

No Rest for the Wicked

"Ozzy — he's like the fucking Energizer Bunny.
He just keeps going, and going,
and going."

KERRY KING, SLAYER

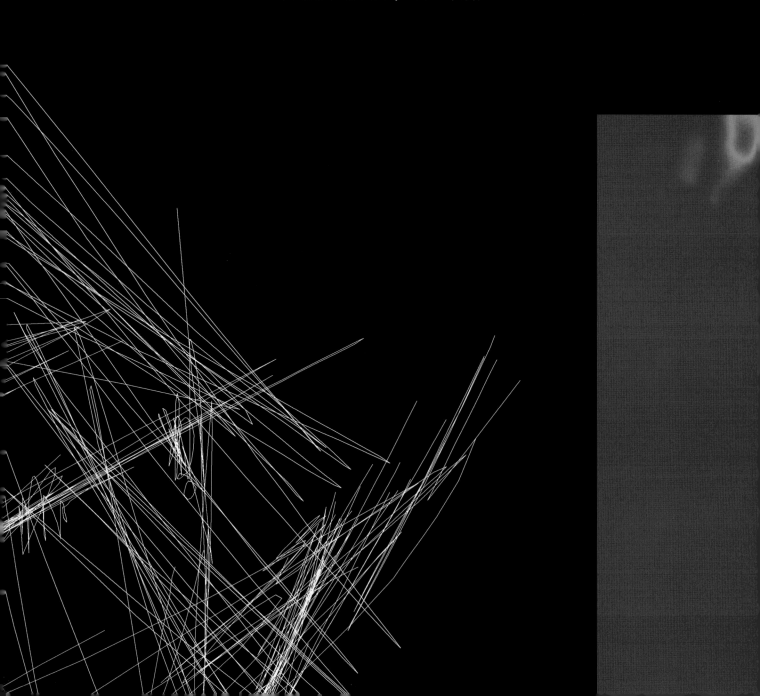

'Ozzy was facing a mutiny. He, Bob Daisley and Jake E Lee had started work on material for *The Ultimate Sin*, following the departure of drummer Tommy Aldridge.

Sharing an apartment with Ozzy, Lee found the singer's unpredictability difficult. Lee's method of working was to stay at home and write songs whereas Ozzy would disappear for whole weekends, or come staggering back in the early hours of the morning and expect the guitarist to get up and start writing on demand. This added to Lee's existing musical frustrations.

During this period, Ozzy spent some time in rehab in one of his frequent attempts to straighten himself out, and was obviously in a fragile condition.

Bob Daisley recalls a furious row: "We were writing a lot in Palm Springs. Jake and I put the music together. Ozzy was in the Betty Ford centre for his alcohol and drug problem. We did some rehearsals and then we were in London to audition drummers...

"We'd been rehearsing and putting the songs together during the week and Ozzy didn't come into some of the rehearsals. When we got into the demos – cos the record company wanted to hear some of the stuff we were doing – he wanted to start changing things, he'd started smoking pot and he was drinking.

"I said, 'Ozzy, look – fucking hell, we've got limited time here. We've got to come up with something to play the record company. Now you want to change stuff... you should've come to rehearsals and we could have done it then.'

"He got all pissed off, and we ended up in an argument. By the end of the night, it was like, 'Fuck you! And you can take fucking Jake with you.' Jake stayed, but I left.

"Then I got a phone call about six weeks after that, saying, 'We've finished the music part of the writing. Will you write the lyrics for the album?'" So I wrote the lyrics for *The Ultimate Sin* at home with tapes that they sent me."

Ozzy recorded the album with Lee, keyboard player Mike Moran and a new rhythm section – bassist Phil Soussan, replacing Daisley, and new drummer Randy Castillo, formerly of Lita Ford's band. Released in February 1986, it was a Top 10 smash in both Britain and America – yet critics, fans and even Ozzy himself agree that it was really a bit of a dog.

Lyrically, it sweeps a familiar landscape, seeking out the common ground between Ozzy and his fan following: hedonism ("Lightning Strikes"), criticism ("Never Know Why"), ruthless ambition (the title track), inner turmoil ("Secret Loser"), psychopathic insanity ("Shot In The Dark") and the threat of nuclear war: "Killer Of Giants" warns that man will destroy the world as a logical result of the arms race, while "Thank God For The Bomb" argues for the nuclear deterrent.

Musically, *The Ultimate Sin* reflects the instability around the band that recorded it. Ozzy plays to the gallery with a slightly subdued bravado, the rock is heavy and the guitar is distorted, grinding and loud but focused and obedient as Lee chops out his chords, riffs and solos. All the songs sound very similar, a layer of Eighties hairspray masking the underlying whiff of ambivalence.

Ozzy blamed producer Ron Nevison, stating: "Although there were good songs on that album, working with a producer like Ron Nevison wasn't a very enjoyable task for me. He changed the whole colour of the album from the way I thought it was going to sound. It was like being in the Boy Scouts... when I think of it, I remember a very sterile environment. I don't have fond memories of that project."

Unhelpfully, censorship raised its head yet again: the original sleeve artwork was pulled because it featured three crucifixes and a knickerless woman. (Prior to this, *Talk Of the Devil* had been stickered in shops because the raspberries coming out of cover-boy Ozzy's mouth looked like clotted blood. He recalled every copy, rather than have the sleeve censored.)

Looking to the future, Ozzy decided that he liked his drummer but could live without the others: Lee and

Scarf-ace Jake comes over all Eighties glam-trash

Soussan both left with harsh words ringing in their ears.

"Phil Soussan was a fucking terrible bass player," blasted Ozzy. "And Jake E Lee was the most miserable man God ever bred...

"If you're living with a miserable fucker who never speaks to you, it spreads through the band like a cancer. When you did a good gig with Jake, you thought you were going to fucking hang yourself."

Jake was less dramatic. Stating that he could no longer tolerate Ozzy's mood swings and the musical restrictions placed upon him, and confirming that his job had become an ordeal, he added: "I also became really disillusioned about the whole music business because of all the shitty things Ozzy said about me in the press."

Meanwhile, Dolores (Dee) Rhoads was being inundated with letters from fans eager to know if there were any plans to release live material featuring her son. She contacted Ozzy, and in May 1987, *Tribute* was released in honour of Randy Rhoads.

Recorded on tour in 1981 with the Ozzy/Rhoads/Sarzo/Aldridge line-up and including Don Airey on keyboards, this was an unusual live album for one reason: it sounded *great*. Serving as a showcase for Rhoads, it caught him at the peak of his playing, turning out the imaginative blend of power, precision, melody, speed, colour and intricacy that was his trademark. It reached number 13 in the charts in Britain and number six in the USA.

Describing *Tribute* as a "beautiful memory", Ozzy revealed that in planning the release with Sharon, he had insisted on only one thing: "Don't put it out at some ludicrous price and with a black album cover showing a guitar leaning against a tombstone."

With Soussan and Lee now out of the picture, Ozzy called Bob Daisley back to the fold, and recruited young guitar wizard Zakk Wylde, who had his own band, Pride And Glory.

Wylde had heard Ozzy mention on the Howard Stern show that he was looking for a guitarist, but didn't dream he might be eligible for the job himself. Later, a mutual photographer friend offered to pass a tape to Ozzy, and Zakk was invited to audition. His arrival brought a new enthusiasm and sense of purpose to the group, and keyboardist John Sinclair, who set about *No Rest For The Wicked* with gusto.

If Ozzy had tested his supporters' loyalties with *Bark At The Moon* and especially *The Ultimate Sin*, this was their reward. The new album marked a convincing return to form: passionately heavy, it offered a

deafening alternative to the glam-rock outfits such as Poison and Guns N' Roses who were packing the stadiums. Released in October 1988, it charted at number 23 in the UK and number 13 in the US.

Ozzy crowed: "Zakk's everything I've been looking for: he's got a great personality, he's dedicated to his instrument and he's just wonderful to have around cos he's always up – he's never down. In rehearsals and that, he'll tell me off sometimes and make me do things, which is just great – he's so different to Jake, who never said anything to anybody... We all communicate like a family and Zakk's only 21, he's brilliant and, let's face it, he'll only get better."

Zakk Wylde

Miracle Man

It was long overdue. Ozzy had been castigated for years by American TV evangelists accusing him of being a Satanist. A rabble-rousing, money-grabbing breed, the preachers were often unmasked as worse sinners than their flocks, and hypocrites to boot.

Like his heroes the Beatles before him, Ozzy saw his albums being destroyed in ritual burnings, *Speak Of The Devil* (the American title) being one which was hurled on the bonfire. He was banned from concert-halls and whole towns, and when he did play, religious fundamentalists would turn up at venues to leaflet the audiences.

A leading Catholic, Cardinal John O'Connor, one-time Archbishop of New York, warned the world that Ozzy was hell's own messenger. One TV evangelist and Ozzy opponent, Oral Roberts, appealed to viewers for $7 million, claiming that God would literally strike him dead if he failed to meet his financial target. Ozzy sent him a dollar – explaining that it should go towards his psychiatric bill.

Then there was Jimmy Swaggart, perhaps the most famous of them all. Keen to denounce Ozzy as a devil's disciple and a parent's nightmare, Swaggart fell from grace spectacularly when he was caught in a hotel with a prostitute. The moral majority was not impressed, despite his tearful, televised pleas to God for forgiveness.

In "Miracle Man", Ozzy takes his revenge on Jimmy Swaggart: "Now Jimmy, he got busted with his pants down/Repent ye wretched sinner, self-righteous clown…"

The first track on the album, it finds Ozzy back on top of things, fully engaged, as Wylde's riff blares out, loud and proud, amid charging tempos.

Devil's Daughter

Ozzy was at it again. "I'll feel your creeping flesh if you're to be possessed/Then I will desecrate what you've become…"

It would be lovely to think that this was intended as an extra "fuck you" to Swaggart, but whatever, the evil aura is compounded by a stuttering vocal with a darkly compelling melodic hook.

"I think that this LP, more than any, has the root of Sabbath in it," explained Ozzy. "And, of course, I think this album's great. I had fun making it, I really did." With "Devil's Daughter", a fired-up rhythm section and a high-powered chorus keep the energy levels of

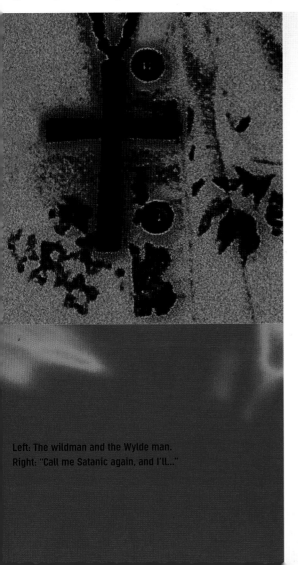

Left: The wildman and the Wylde man.
Right: "Call me Satanic again, and I'll…"

"Miracle Man" cracking on, while the flamboyant lead guitar and robust rhythm play bear out the first impressions: Zakk Wylde was a Good Thing.

A musician with special interests in Southern-fried boogie and country rock as well as heavy metal, he took to his new guitar-hero role intuitively. "As far as me and Zakk are concerned, I'm proud to have discovered a new talent," declared Ozzy. "The most rewarding thing is remembering this raggedy-arsed kid walking through the door and ultimately becoming this great guy. And Zakk Wylde is a great fucking guy!"

He added: "You need young guys – why should I want old farts around me? I'm old enough. But having young guys in the band keeps me young. It keeps me in touch with what the kids are about... I'd much rather have young musicians with me than when you look to the back of the stage and see all those bald patches... and the older generation don't buy the records like the younger kids do."

Ozzy realized how easily he could intimidate his more junior recruits: "For the first month, it's very hard for new guys because they all believe what they've read in the papers. They think I'm a lunatic with an axe who runs around chopping people's heads off all day. I'm not like that at all!"

BLOODBATH IN PARADISE

On the evening of August 9, 1969, a band of disciples of insane cult leader Charles Manson went to a house at 10050 Cielo Drive, Beverly Hills, and murdered all the occupants. The assassins – three women and a man – knew who lived at the address, but that wasn't important. They selected the mansion because it was isolated. Their frenzied attacks left four victims with 102 stab wounds; the fifth victim was shot.

Sharon Tate, who was eight months pregnant and shared the home with her husband, film director Roman Polanski, was tied up and slaughtered in the living room, as was the internationally successful hair stylist Jay Sebring. Outside, coffee heiress Abigail Folger and her boyfriend Voytek Frykowski were slumped on the ground, alongside the body of Steve Parent, a young man who had arrived in his car to visit the caretaker. He was gunned down with a .22 calibre pistol. Jay Sebring and Voytek Frykowski were shot too. Parent

and Frykowski were also bludgeoned around the head. On a door, the word "pig" was written in blood.

After midnight, the Manson Family members set out again, this time with their leader. They arrived at 3301 Waverly Drive and butchered husband and wife Leno and Rosemary LaBianca, stabbing them a total of 67 times and carving the word "war" into Leno's stomach. More slogans were daubed in blood around the house – "death to pigs" and "rise". Infamously, the mis-spelt "healther skelter" glared violently from the fridge door.

The atrocities which shocked America have been revisited in songs ever since, and this is Ozzy's.

"Can you hear them in the darkness?/Helter skelter, spiral madness (yeah)", torments the singer, returning

Dry-ice dramatics

Ozzy on the "endless road"

Manson and his sidekicks to a decent society where they can again cause carnage and terror – in our nightmares. Not content with reintroducing Manson as a modern-day bogeyman, Ozzy added a mischievous touch: a backwards-playing message.

He revealed: "You know on the beginning of 'Blood Bath In Paradise' – all those weird noises and that weird talking? That's all a big joke. If you play it backwards, it says, 'Your mother sells whelks in Hull'. I'm still waiting for some dickhead to pick up on that and tell people I'm sending messages to the Devil." Some dickhead undoubtedly did.

Meanwhile, Ozzy was inviting trouble with the video for another album track, "Crazy Babies", a song about children born to mothers on crack. It was banned.

"There must be some sick people working for these censorship boards," he raved. "They must be a bunch of perverts to read anything into that video. It makes me

sick. I mean, if I had a pair of tits and my name was Madonna, they wouldn't have blinked an eye."

He whizzed on: "I could release a version of 'My Way' and somebody in America would find something to read into it, something disgusting." Ozzy concluded: "It's not me you have to worry about. It's all of them – the PMRC who try to ban the shows and the fucking sheriff in Texas who says he can't guarantee my safety if I show my face in town. These are the people that cause all the trouble in America. I don't have to lift a finger."

Demon Alcohol

Ozzy was struggling with his addictions to drink and drugs. By now, he was able to admit freely that he had a problem, but despite his valiant attempts to clean up and dry out, he was still a few years away from winning the war.

happy-pissed, I go bulldozing around. I don't even know what I'm doing or where I'm at. Sharon says she's terrified when she sees me drink now. It upsets the whole family, close friends and everybody that works for me."

He added: "I've fucked up so many things through drugs and drink... I was like a mad dog chasing my tail... I've polluted every cell in my body with this crap, so my body gets pissed off when it can't get it."

Ozzy confided that he'd become "a fit-drinker", going into spasms during withdrawal, which is why he had originally sought proper detox treatment at the Betty Ford clinic and had joined AA to try and control his desires. One popular story insists that on his first visit to Betty Ford's, Ozzy believed he was going there to learn to drink in moderation – and immediately checked out on discovering that there was no bar.

"I met Betty Ford a couple of times," he remembered later. "She was a very quiet lady. She'd come in like royalty, have the unit polished. She was all right, though. She'd hover like a blow-up doll at one end of the wing and then go out the other. It was, like, 13 Hail Bettys and she'd go home."

Finally: "You name it, I drank it, from whisky to gin and cider. I didn't care if I lived or died."

Other tracks on the album are the rocking fan favourite "Crazy Babies"; "Breaking All The Rules", an incitement to have the courage of your convictions; "Fire In The Sky" (hopefully not a Deep Purple reference!), which emerges from an atmospheric synth intro to explore the effects of childhood trauma upon the grown adult; the infectious "Tattooed Dancer", introducing the dominating, "mean, hard woman" who knows what she wants; and the hidden bonus track, "Hero".

Tracks on *Tribute* are: "I Don't Know", "Crazy Train", "Believer", "Mr Crowley", "Flying High Again", "Revelation (Mother Earth)", "Steal Away (The Night)", "Suicide Solution", "Iron Man", "Children Of The Grave", "Paranoid", "Goodbye To Romance", "No Bone Movies" and "Dee".

Tracks on *The Ultimate Sin* are: "The Ultimate Sin", "Secret Loser", "Never Know Why", "Thank God For The Bomb", "Never", "Lightning Strikes", "Killer Of Giants", "Fool Like You" and "Shot In the Dark".

"Demon Alcohol" – a song that sounds as tough as Ozzy's drinking capacity – was and remains a warning, a testament to the seductiveness of booze. It's definitely Ozzy's song, whether or not Bob Daisley wrote or co-wrote the words.

"I'll watch you lose control, consume your very soul," says the bottle to the singer, later referring back to the controversial Blizzard Of Ozz track: "Don't speak of suicide solutions, you took my hand, I'm here to stay".

Ozzy's public stance on drinking had changed over the years. Once, he was challenging: "I get high. I get fucked up. What the hell's wrong with getting fucked up?"

But now he was facing the fact that things had gone too far, stating in true AA style: "All I know is, I am an alcoholic and my name is Ozzy. And I've gotta take certain steps to try and arrest the disease. Because I'm either gonna kill myself, kill someone else or I'm gonna go insane... It's got to the point now where I don't get

NO MORE TEARS

"Ozzy is king!"
MIKE MUSHOK, STAIND

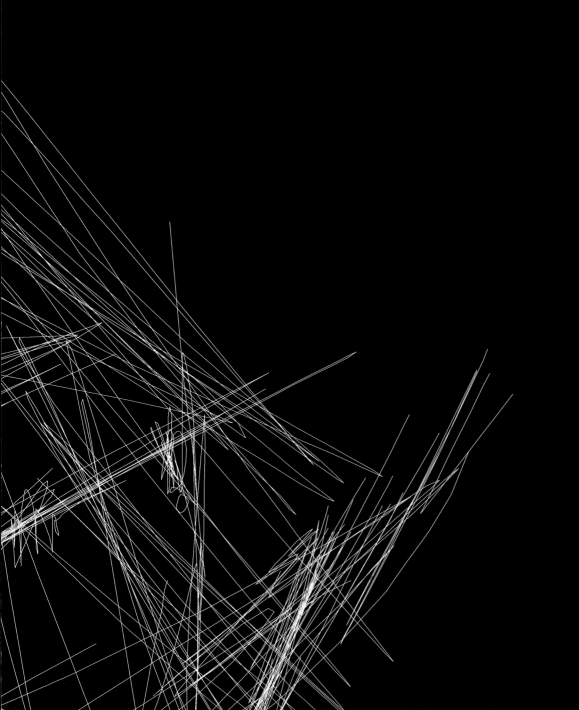

At the end of 1988, Ozzy set out on the road to promote *No Rest For The Wicked* with a familiar figure on bass. Black Sabbath's Geezer Butler stepped in for the tour (commemorated on the live mini-album, *Just Say Ozzy*, which was released to little acclaim in February 1990).

Ozzy's on-off efforts to quit booze and drugs were definitely off again. By the time the band stepped on to a plane at Newark bound for the Moscow Music Peace Festival in 1989, Ozzy was tired and emotional... and in need of the toilet.

He was billed alongside Bon Jovi, Motley Crüe, Skid Row, Cinderella, The Scorpions and Gorky Park for the Soviet Union's first major rock concert by Western artists.

The extravaganza, held in August in the Lenin Stadium, was staged by the Make A Difference Foundation, who, in conjunction with producers and organizers in the US and the USSR, were promoting international co-operation on fighting drug abuse among young people.

Journalist Adam Curry was on the flight with all of the artists. He wrote: "Ozzy was totally hammered... So I'm sitting with Geezer, shooting the Sabbath shit, when Ozzy starts mumbling loudly near the rear bulkhead."

The girlfriend of Bon Jovi drummer Tico Torres was in the toilet – and Ozzy couldn't or wouldn't wait his turn.

"I looked up to see Ozzy standing spreadeagled in the aisle, with a huge, dark spot in his crotch area and a growing pool of urine at his feet," wrote Curry. "What was funny was how both Sharon and Geezer acted as if they witnessed this type of behaviour daily. Sharon even had a change of clothes for Ozzy in her carry-on."

Ozzy was infamous for his spontaneous leaks – the Alamo simply being the most controversial. He had also showered Hitler's memorial in Berlin, had relieved himself out of a venue window not realizing that fans were queuing just below, and had been interviewed by the FBI over rumours that he intended to pee on the steps of the White House.

Sharon was indeed used to all this, turning a blind eye to Ozzy's "idiosyncrasies" while ruling his career with a rod of iron. She had often supported her husband's more outrageous antics because of their publicity value, and had been suspected by many of orchestrating the incident where he bit the head off a dove in the offices of CBS/Epic Records.

Yet, she could be formidable if she thought things had gone too far. There are stories of Sharon punching groupies and fighting Ozzy with her bare fists or any other handy object as she struggled to keep him away from cocaine. It seemed that she was coming out on top.

In 1988, Ozzy had said: "I'm John Osbourne now... You've got no fear of me being fucking Ozzy Osbourne around here – because if I am, Sharon goes, 'Fuck off. Go and soak your head in the horse trough and don't come back until you've found your brains.'"

But shortly after the Moscow festival – on September

"Your mother sells whelks in Hull!"

2, 1989 – Ozzy started drinking heavily at home, flew into a violent rage and tried to strangle Sharon while snarling a warning: "We've decided that you've got to go." She hit the alarm system's panic button.

What started as a family celebration for daughter Aimee's sixth birthday ended with Ozzy being frog-marched off by the police and charged with attempted murder.

He said: "I mixed some medication I'd been prescribed by a psychiatrist with alcohol and I just blacked out. I woke up the next day in Amersham police station, and I honestly didn't know what was going on. The copper said, 'Do you know why you're here?' and they told me I'd threatened to kill my wife." He also admitted: "I don't remember anything. I was *gone*. I went to court and everything, but she dropped the charges."

Pleading temporary insanity, Ozzy – horrified by what he had done – was ordered by the court to go into rehab at Huntercombe Manor, in England. He spent three months there.

"But I came out, I drank again, I couldn't stop... I was a mess." Finally, said Ozzy, "All that craziness stopped once I put the cork back into the bottle."

Ozzy entered the Nineties on Prozac and an exercise

bike, and with a new, healthy diet – no red meat, no raw animals. Then he went back to work.

No More Tears is often described as Ozzy's first sober album, and it has been hailed as one of his finest. A mixture of ballads and pounding rockers of consistently high quality, it's an album he made to satisfy himself and nobody else.

Pre-production work began with Zakk Wylde, Randy Castillo and bass player Mike Inez (later to join Alice In Chains), who initiated the title track. Legendary Motorhead mainman Lemmy helped out with the lyrics for "I Don't Want To Change The World", "Desire" and "Hellraiser" and wrote all the words for "Mama, I'm Coming Home".

When it came to recording time, Bob Daisley's phone rang. "Mike was Ozzy's bass player at the time," Daisley told Jeb Wright. "I got a call from Ozzy and he said he was having problems getting the songs recorded and he asked me to come down and give it a try. I played on the whole album. Mike Inez got credit as playing some bass on it but he didn't do any of it... I had great fun doing it. I got involved with the lyrics, but they didn't use them. They used my lyrics to inspire other lyrics to be written... I just played on that one." It

An unusual peacefulness descends

was Daisley's last work on an Ozzy album.

The album was released in October 1991. It charted at number 17 in the UK and was a resounding number seven hit in the US.

Everything was looking up for the cleaned-up, slimmed-down Ozzy Osbourne. And then, perversely, he announced his retirement – and a No More Tours tour.

MR TINKERTRAIN

Kicking off the album in controversial style, "Mr Tinkertrain" adopts the creepy persona of a paedophile who abducts a young child: "I've got the kind of toys you've never seen... Little angel, come and sit upon my knee."

"Fuck knows where that came from," commented Daisley.

Naturally, Ozzy came in for some flak, not just for tackling a taboo subject in the first place but also for the song's explicit depiction of an imaginary scenario involving the man and his victim.

There were, however, some very unexpected reactions,

with one reviewer describing it as a "fun song" with "comedic" lyrics, a classic example of Ozzy's "humorous side".

Generally, listeners took the view that the language was too simplistic and the vision too narrow to make anything other than the most banal protest against child abuse.

Lyrics apart, "Mr Tinkertrain" is a storming rock track, Zakk Wylde riffing madly as if briefly consumed by the spirit of AC/DC. Wylde enjoyed the recording sessions enormously, having gained in confidence and capability. He confided to writer Gary Graff: "On the first album [*No Rest For The Wicked*]... Ozzy didn't even know if I could cut it. He was more or less constantly over my shoulder going, 'This sounds like Jimi Hendrix, don't do that,' or, 'Zakk, just sound like yourself.' But at the time I didn't even know who the fuck I was or what my fucking sound was. I knew I liked playing Les Pauls through Marshall amps and playing pentatonic scales."

By the time of *No More Tears,* Wylde said, "I had done a record, done a tour and I was happy with the songs we had. So it was more relaxed. Ozzy felt it too; he gave me more freedom that time out."

I Don't Want to Change the World

Ozzy: "I won a Grammy for this one. The song's meaning is self-explanatory, in respect that lines like, 'Tell me I'm a sinner, I've got news for you'... well, it's kind of a spoof on me, you know."

A smart retort to the enemy – any enemy – the track picks up and runs with the vigorous rockability of "Mr Tinkertrain". Co-written by Lemmy, Ozzy, Wylde and Castillo, it was awarded a Grammy in 1993 for Best Metal Performance.

According to Zakk Wylde, the band knew they were on to a good thing in the studio, but they didn't know how good. They could not have realized that they were producing Grammy-quality material, or that the album would be such a hit in the US.

Wylde told Gary Graff: "It's like a Salvador Dali painting. He didn't sit around and go, 'I'm gonna paint this today. It's gonna be my most famous one.' If he got inspired, he painted it. If we get inspired, we just write it and record it. You just get lucky, man."

The atmosphere in the sessions was certainly indicative of a band that were feeling happy and creative. Recording first at Bearsville Studios in New York and later relocating to LA, they exchanged a series of malodorous practical jokes instigated by Ozzy, who cracked a stink bomb in the room shared by Wylde and Castillo.

As the tit-for-tat continued, the stink bombs gave way to something altogether more solid and messy. "We had a blast when we were up there," chuckled Wylde.

Ozzy later paid an appropriate tribute to Lemmy, an old friend: "I always think of Lemmy when I see a can of Carlsberg Special... it's great stuff if you want a night out on the booze. The trick isn't to start early on in the evening with it, but later on when you're ready to collapse. You don't last very long with this stuff, it's so strong – and that's speaking from experience."

Mama, I'm Coming Home

Although it's generally accepted that Lemmy penned the lyrics, he did so expressly for the man who would sing them. The title comes from Ozzy's regular phone call home to "Mama", his pet name for Sharon, as the end of each tour drew near.

The sentiments of the song, in part, seem quite appropriate: "I've seen your face a hundred times/Every day we've been apart." In other lines, a fictitious element arises, with a submissive lover returning, tail between legs, to a lying, flint-hearted woman.

Clearly, this is no reflection of the relationship between Ozzy and Sharon which, despite its temptestuous rows, was and is based on real love, respect and teamwork, with each understanding and offering the qualities needed by the other.

Musically, it's a dramatic and tuneful ballad which progresses from Wylde's acoustic picking and emphatic chording to a spot of jamming and a climactic finish built up by backing vocals. Bob Daisley singles it out as one which was "fun to do" on his fretless bass.

No More Tears

Reportedly recorded as a post-script to the sessions – as "Paranoid" had been – "No More Tears" was originally titled "Say Hello To Heaven". A portrait of a serial killer stalking prostitutes, it vividly describes the man in the dark, his parting kiss on the cold lips of a victim, and an additional twist of insanity: "I never wanted it to end this way my love, my darling/Believe me when I say to you in love I think I'm falling here..."

The seven-minute musical adventure starts out with a bassline much beloved of Ozzy fans and carries on through a progression of sounds and styles that includes a Beatles-flavoured middle section. A call-and-response exchange between Zakk's guitar and Ozzy's vocals is prominently featured, while synths, keyboards and a moody piano add to the atmospheric impact. And it rocks, too.

A real team effort credited to Ozzy, Wylde, Castillo, Michael Inez and co-producer John Purdell, it was one of those songs that sprang to life by accident – just like old times.

Ozzy: doing the Zombie Stomp

Zakk Wylde recalled: "Ozzy started singing the melody, and I just played that Tony Iommi-esque riff with the flat fives in there. I had my slide in my hand too, so I worked out some stuff with that."

Bob Daisley remembers that the song was a fait accompli by the time he arrived to take over the bass duties. He said: "Mike Inez used to come and watch me play in the studio. I found him to be a very friendly guy. Mike had the idea of starting the song with the bass and he had an intro that he had written. I changed it around a bit when I came in."

Ozzy with trademark cross: "a terrible old showbiz ham"

"There's no such thing as moderation in Ozzy Osbourne's vocabulary... It's all or nothing — whether it's drugs, sex, drink, falling in love, anything."

Zombie Stomp

A song about the nature of addiction, "Zombie Stomp" sums up Ozzy's countless but finally successful efforts to quit his vices.

"Hey, hey, do the zombie stomp/Thinkin' how it could have been if I had never let them in..."

Said Ozzy: "For many years I was trying to stop the booze and I couldn't stop it, man, it was like a monkey on my back. I'm not one of those holier-than-thou fuckers either. Believe me, if I thought I could successfully go to the fridge and get a can of beer and have a good old fucking laugh, then I would. But I know if I go to that beer then I'm fucking over. One's too many and ten's not enough."

He has also insisted: "There's not enough alcohol in the world for me. There's no such thing as moderation in Ozzy Osbourne's vocabulary... It's all or nothing – whether it's drugs, sex, drink, falling in love, anything."

He wasn't joking: "Back then it was two cases of Dom Perignon, a case of Hennessey... beer, drugs, everything. I was doing four bottles of brandy a day and as much cocaine, pot and champagne as I could handle. I was out of control." That was as well as the morphine, Demerol, Valium, barbiturates and steroids.

"Everyone blames rock'n'roll for their problems," reflected Ozzy. "But let me tell you the truth. It's a great way to make a living. But if you want to be an idiot and take bags of drugs and drink, you will die. I've tried the lot and I'm not proud of it."

He saw tragedy strike down his friends and colleagues: "It was terribly sad so many stars died, just for the sake of silliness. I'm no better than John Bonham or Keith Moon, just luckier."

Then there was Def Leppard's Steve Clark: "He didn't drink for pleasure. He drank to escape. He had too much too soon and couldn't cope. He had it all – talent, nice houses and cars. Now he's dead at 30."

"A lot of my drinking friends died in their forties – heart attacks," Ozzy expanded. "One guy's liver exploded. There but for the grace of God go I. There must be a guiding star over me."

Ozzy's efforts to get on the wagon and stay there would invariably come to grief when touring time rolled around again, with the easily obtained drugs and drinks holding out the offer of some fun, some familiarity, a sense of camaraderie and a relief from the pressures, the relentless grind of travelling and the boring hours spent just hanging around.

In the end, it was not the attack on Sharon, or the deaths of his friends, that saw Ozzy sober up; it was a moment of personal realization.

He said: "I just couldn't stand it any more – the shakes, the horrors, the phone ringing thinking, 'Fuck, it's bad news,' and that horrible feeling of blacking out..."

He added: "I was frightened of living and frightened of dying, and that's a horrible place to be. I just didn't have the bottle to end it. I'd wake up in the morning and if I didn't have anything to worry about, I'd worry. And it would escalate into this incredible dark monster in my head, and the only escape I used to know was drugs and booze."

Told by a psychiatrist that he had a chemical imbalance in the brain caused by his over-indulgences, Ozzy was put on the anti-depressant Prozac and prescribed anti-seizure medication. He's resigned to the fact that he'll have to keep on taking the tablets, struggling with the demons and, probably, visiting his therapist for the rest of his life.

Other tracks on the album are the tough "Desire", a commitment to keep on rocking; the heavy-duty "S.I.N." (Shadows In The Night), which opens, in archetypal Ozzy style, with the words: "A psycho driver twisted in my head/Silence broken, but there's nothing said"; the rollicking "Hellraiser", pouring out clichés about the heroic rock'n'roller on the "endless road"; "Time After Time", a love-lorn softie; the hard and heavy "A.V.H.", apparently an abbreviation for Aston Villa Highway and not the rumoured "alcohol, valium and hash", despite the suggestions of its lyrics; and the country-coloured "Road To Nowhere", the third and final ballad which would seem to look back on Ozzy's life. The remastered version of the album includes two extra tracks – "Don't Blame Me", the B-side of the "Mama, I'm Coming Home" single, and "Party With the Animals", from the soundtrack to "Buffy The Vampire Slayer".

The tracks on the preceding mini-album, *Just Say Ozzy*, are "Miracle Man", "Bloodbath In Paradise", "Shot In The Dark", "Tattooed Dancer", "Sweet Leaf" and "War Pigs".

Staring into the abyss: a chemically unbalanced Ozzy Osbourne

Ozzmosis

"Ozzy is one of heavy metal's leading innovators, and his Ozzfest tours have definitely made metal more popular."
DAVE BAKSH,
SUM 41

"I'm a happily married man with three kids that I absolutely adore..."

There were those who thought that Ozzy's "retirement" would never last. And there were those who thought he never meant it in the first place, that it was a ploy to sell more albums and tour tickets. This viewpoint was reinforced on the final night of the No More Tours tour, at Costa Mesa, California in November 1992. Climaxing with a four-song Black Sabbath reunion, the gig ended with a spectacular fireworks display which reportedly spelt out the message, "I'll be back."

Despite this, Ozzy seemed initially genuine in his desire to step out of public life. It was easier to avoid the temptations of drink and drugs when he was at home. He was becoming prone to illness and injury and was fed up with touring. And he wanted to spend time with Sharon and their three children, Aimee (born on September 2, 1983), Kelly (born October 27, 1984) and Jack (born November 8, 1985).

But Ozzy's idyllic vision of a future filled with domesticity and school sports days was doomed to be disappointing.

"I went home, gained a stack of weight, bought

The joys of family life tempted Ozzy into retirement – for five minutes

motorcycles and guns and all this other shit," said Ozzy. "Then I started doing things I'd always wanted to do. I bought a football and played football with my son. I really enjoyed being a dad... for about a week. Then Sharon said to me one day, 'Is that it now? Are you finished?' She let me get all these things out of my system. Then she asked me what I wanted to do. And I said, 'I want to get a band, man.'" Ozzy was coming back.

"I never really went into retirement as such," he later confessed. "I mean, I'm always making these stupid, dumb fucking statements and then I wonder, 'What the fuck did I say that for?' I wanted to know what it was like to be off, not to be living on a schedule. I did the No More Tours tour and then I wondered, 'What the fuck do I do now? What is retirement?'"

During his absence, Ozzy had authorized the release of a double album, *Live and Loud*, recorded during the farewell tour with henchmen Wylde, Castillo and Inez. Issued in June 1993, it didn't bother the UK chart, although it reached a reasonable number 22 in the US.

Returning to the fray in 1994, Ozzy intended to make a fresh start with a new band, but there were lots of twists and turns before a line-up and production team were finally assembled.

The musicians originally answering his calls were guitarist Steve Vai, drummer Dean Castronovo and the reliable Bob Daisley. Ozzy and Vai wrote songs together and work began in Vai's LA studio before the singer decided that the partnership wasn't really working.

Ozzy said: "While Steve never treated me like anything less than a gentleman and I was fine with him, it was felt that maybe I should work with actual songwriters."

With Vai out of the picture, Ozzy recalled Zakk Wylde to the band. He also brought Geezer Butler in on bass. Bob Daisley said: "I thought, 'Oh fuck, thanks a lot.'"

The band that recorded the comeback album, *Ozzmosis* (originally titled *X-Ray*), comprised Wylde, Butler and Castronovo, with Rick Wakeman and producer Michael Beinhorn both contributing on keyboards. Beinhorn had been invited to replace *No More Tears* producers Duane Baron and John Purdell, who'd started work on the new album. Ozzy scrapped those recordings.

Ozzy had also been teaming up with various songwriters, first Mark Hudson and Steve Dudas, and then Jim Vallance. As a result, he had a whole host of co-writers for the album – Vai, Wylde, Purdell, Baron,

Guitar maestro Steve Vai teamed up with Ozzy. It didn't last...

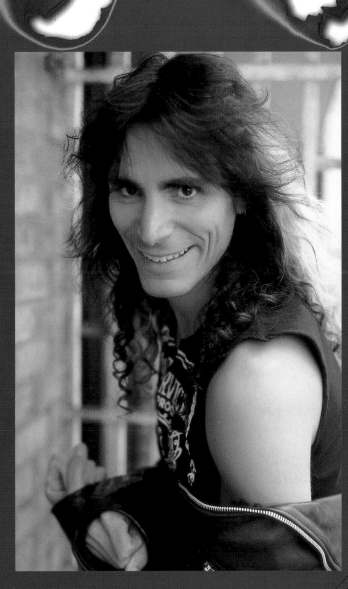

Vallance, Hudson, Dudas, Butler and, on "See You On The Other Side", Lemmy.

Released in October 1995, *Ozzmosis* was an enormous hit in the US, peaking at number 4 (number 22 in the UK), but it doesn't sound quite as Ozzy had intended, which was "very fucking heavy".

Granted, it has heavy elements, but the keyboard arrangements and the ballads contribute to a more sophisticated result, and Ozzy himself later admitted to regretting the "sterile" sound.

Lyrically, there are some tender moments, but most of the tracks dwell on familiar topics, namely death and the afterlife. "Every time I try to get out of the darkness, it drags me back," sighed Ozzy.

The tour was called Retirement Sucks, and it hit the road without Zakk Wylde, who'd been in talks about a job with Guns N' Roses and wasn't sure if he'd be available. He agreed to give Ozzy his final decision on a certain date, but failed to call. Ozzy said: "All I wanted was a straight answer from him – but he didn't show me that respect."

Joe Holmes "plays like a motherfucker".

Always on the lookout for a bright, new talent, Ozzy spotted a guitarist who "plays like a motherfucker". That was Joe Holmes. Holmes, who had previously worked with Dave Lee Roth, was a pupil of Randy Rhoads. Rhoads, while on tour, would himself take classical guitar tuition, and would also arrange workshops in which he gave lessons to young players.

"It's really spooky," said Ozzy, "because when Joe plays the Randy Rhoads stuff, he plays just like him – it's like I can see Randy's fingers." He added: "I love giving guys a break and watching them develop. And they all develop, they all get egos, they all get pissed off and after that, they all fly from the nest. And then I get another one."

In a final line-up change, Geezer Butler left the tour half way through, suffering from homesickness, making way for Mike Inez to come back.

Ozzy and Sharon, meanwhile, were beginning to realize that they did not have to become slaves to the time-honoured album-tour-album-tour cycle. They were making plans for their own label, the short-lived Ozz Records, and for a heavy metal extravaganza they called the Ozzfest.

Ozzy said: "I was talking to Sharon... and she said that since radio and MTV had stopped playing our type of music, I, as one of the founding forefathers of what they call 'metal', should do something for the people that still like it."

Ozzfest started as a two-day event in America in September 1996, with Ozzy headlining a bill that encompassed the best of the era's big bands including Slayer, Sepultura, Fear Factory and Biohazard and a spread of then up-and-coming acts such as Coal Chamber, Cellophane, Earth Crisis and Powerman 5000.

"... one of the founding forefathers of what they call 'metal'..."

Adding to the atmosphere was a variety of sideshows and booths for tattoos and body-piercing.

With 50,000 tickets sold across the two dates, the Ozzfest fulfilled its potential immediately. It would then mushroom into an annual, international touring package that would rehabilitate Ozzy as a major live attraction, a living legend, and a godfather and benefactor of heavy metal.

PERRY MASON

Information filtering out from the studio where Ozzy and the band were working "very, very hard" with producer Michael Beinhorn, said that the album would be unremittingly heavy.

"There's no turning back now," announced Ozzy. "I've lived with these songs for a long time. And if you think I'm bad now, wait until the mix, wait until the mastering! I'll wanna kill everybody!"

He also insisted: "No more 'Goodbye To Romance' or 'Mama, I'm Coming Home' – that's all fuckin' dead and history, man!" Eventually, the brief did widen, and the album was completed with its share of ballads and musical layering.

However, "Perry Mason", which launches the album with tremendous force, survives as evidence of Ozzy's intentions, along with "Thunder Underground" and "My Jekyll Doesn't Hide", both co-written with Zakk Wylde and Geezer Butler.

"Perry Mason", written by Ozzy, Wylde and John Purdell, carries the combined clout of Wylde's heavy guitar riffing, Geezer's rumbling bass and a synthesizer arrangement, and it immortalizes the famous TV lawyer played by Raymond Burr.

The name came first – Ozzy scribbled it down as a potential title – and the lyrics were written to fit, opening, typically enough, with a murder. "Who can we get on the case?/We need Perry Mason..."

I JUST WANT YOU

"I wrote this song with Jim Vallance in his studio in Canada," said Ozzy. "It was one of those magical days when everything seemed to be working. We sat there and came up with these incredible lines – 'There are no impossible dreams/There are no invisible seams'... And after all those incredible things said in the song, the one line, 'I don't ask much, I just want you,' seemed to be a nice way to sum it all up."

Ozzy was enjoying the experience of working with professional songwriters. He recalled: "I've always worked in a band environment where we just jam through stuff and work things out as we go. Previously, the band would spend the first two hours talking about what they were up to last night, how many chicks they got a blow job off, how many beers they'd drunk, how many titty bars they'd been to... working with real songwriters is a whole learning process for both parties."

He added: "I was first paired with Mark Hudson and Steve Dudas and I was amazed at how quickly it was coming out... I've had a lot of fun with them on the way, too – and while I won't be using all the stuff we wrote, I'll be keeping a good part of it. Then came the Jim Vallance thing. Jim and I really learned a lot off each other."

"I Just Want You" takes a measured pace, and again features the synth, but a big guitar sound and a thumping rhythm section pack a solid punch. The track became a great favourite through its exposure on MTV.

SEE YOU ON THE OTHER SIDE

Ozzy, Zakk and Lemmy together came up with one of Ozzy's most personal songs about death and the afterlife. Much was made of the fact that this ballad was written after American comedian Sam Kinnison died in a head-on car smash and Steve Marriott, former Small Faces and Humble Pie frontman, was burnt to death in a bedroom fire.

But Ozzy himself explained: "I wrote that song for my wife. I absolutely adore my wife. The love that I have for her and the love she has for me will never die. I truly believe that if I pop off first or she goes, then we'll meet

Steve Marriott: died tragically wrong

up on the other side. I believe in life after death, which is strange because at one point, I didn't believe in life after birth.

"I believe in life after death because I'm getting closer to it now and I'm at the half-way point at least! It's like a message to Sharon because I love her."

Sharon has been quoted as saying: "Ozzy wrote that song when he was really ill earlier this year and he was being wrongly diagnosed. He was told that he had an illness that was really bad and we thought that that was it, that he was going to die. That's where it came from."

A new poignancy now surrounds the song with the news of Sharon's battle against cancer and Ozzy's worried revelation: "I've done a lot of praying, believe it or not."

This is widely considered to be the best of the album's slow songs with its metal-edged melody and some expressive guitar work from Wylde.

My Little Man

Once again choosing a subject close to his heart, Ozzy declares his devotion to his son Jack. Now an unlikely sex symbol through his TV exposure on "The Osbournes", the gawky and accident-prone Jack was almost ten at the time *Ozzmosis* was released.

"Don't you know that I love you more than life itself," sings Ozzy, with unashamed pride and tenderness. "I'd like to keep you with me all your life but I know I can't do that."

The blatant sentimentality of the lyrics, coupled with the relatively gentle musical environment, irritated many fans. Others were happy to discover a soft side to Ozzy's personality, and they have pointed to the harnessed power of the band and a cracking Wylde guitar solo as redeeming qualities.

It is also thought that the slow but darker album track "Denial" addresses Ozzy's confused relationship with Jessica, his daughter by first wife Thelma.

"My Little Man" was one of the songs that came from Ozzy's partnership with Steve Vai, who claims that the singer originally planned to use both him and Zakk Wylde on the album but that his contributions were vetoed by the record company.

He told Steven Rosen that in his writing sessions with Ozzy, "we got some great, great stuff." He added, "After I met Ozzy, I really started to like him a lot. He was a lot of fun all the time... He's really a pretty wild guy."

One proud dad and one little man

Old LA Tonight

Reportedly written around the time of the LA riots, "Old LA Tonight" is usually interpreted as being a song about home and hearth, bringing the album to a tranquil end with evocative, Rick Wakeman piano, synth and guitar play – a sound which again divided the fans.

While admitting to a vulnerability and uncertainty about the future, the song exhibits a positive element, with a one-day-at-a-time hopefulness about the choruses: "It's gonna be all right in old LA tonight."

Ozzy has been shuttling between LA and England for years with his family, his blunt Brummie wit somehow weathering the Hollywood humour by-pass.

He said: "I love it here, although I don't think I could ever live full-time in the US. The thing about going back to England is that it's quieter and calmer and I can

"The great thing about LA is that everyone minds their own business. Apart from Sharon not getting on with the neighbours."

collect myself more easily. As it happens, Malibu is one of my favourite places ever – better than Hawaii, better than anywhere in the States."

He also enthused: "The great thing about LA is that everyone minds their own business. Apart from Sharon not getting on with the neighbours." And another "bonus": "If anyone gets into my house out there, I would have no hesitation in blowing his head off. I've never kept a gun in the house in England, but I will keep one in LA."

"One" would seem a modest tally...

With the *Ozzmosis* album, and tracks like "Old LA Tonight", Ozzy finally showed his hand as a home-loving, family man – at least since he sobered up – as well as a TV addict who loves nothing more than a night in front of the History and Discovery channels.

He said: "I've come to the conclusion that people don't want to know the truth – that I'm a happily married man with three kids that I absolutely adore, and that what I do is entertain people. I am not fucking Dracula."

With "The Osbournes", Ozzy would learn that millions of people finally did want to know the truth.

Other tracks on the album are the mellow and persuasively melodic "Ghost Behind My Eyes", which describes a nightmarish torment; and the haunting "Tomorrow", a moody track punctuated with clamorous choruses, while Ozzy's treated vocals add an effective peculiarity to the mix.

Tracks on the preceding *Live and Loud* album are: "Intro", "Paranoid", "I Don't Want To Change The World", "Desire", "Mr Crowley", "I Don't Know", "Road To Nowhere", "Flying High Again", "Guitar Solo", "Suicide Solution", "Goodbye To Romance", "Shot In The Dark", "No More Tears", "Miracle Man", "Drum Solo", "War Pigs", "Bark At The Moon", "Mama, I'm Coming Home", "Crazy Train", "Black Sabbath" and "Changes".

Down to Earth

"Ozzy's just a really sweet guy. He's still got a great sense of humour, he still loves touring and he's still out there rocking. And the fact that he got a star on the Hollywood Walk of Fame is hilarious, because Ozzy's the prototypical bad kid/rock star, regardless of how hard he tries to keep himself together."

SLASH, EX-GUNS N' ROSES GUITARIST

Still touring after all these years

It would be half-a-dozen years before Ozzy got around to recording another solo album. He did keep the home fires burning with the release in November 1997 of *The Ozzman Cometh*, a best-of collection featuring studio and live material. But Ozzy was otherwise busy with the growing Ozzfest – and with various Black Sabbath reunions.

The first one had taken place at the Philadelphia leg of the giant Live Aid fund-raiser on July 13, 1985, an event that Ozzy felt coerced into joining. He said at the time, "If I back out, I'll be the only artist in the world to turn around and say, 'Fuck it.'"

In 1989, he barked: "I will never rejoin Black Sabbath. No fucking way! Not in this life or the next…"

And in 1990, he declared: "This whole black cloud had followed us again," adding, "It was over – the cement was on the fucking box. That was when I knew there'd never be a chance of us getting back together." Just a year later, however, serious talks began about the possibility of an organized reunion, but they fell apart in a flurry of arguments among the members' different representatives.

By November 1992, relations were thawing. Ozzy and Sabbath were again onstage together during the last date of the singer's "farewell" tour in Costa Mesa, California.

Then came Ozzfest 1997. Ozzy, Tony Iommi and Geezer Butler came together with ex-Faith No More drummer Mike Bordin to close the show, playing for roughly an hour after Ozzy's solo set. Bill Ward – by then clean and sober – was devastated not to be invited. According to Sharon Osbourne, this was due to, "interpersonal business conflicts between himself, me and Ozzy".

Bill was back on the drum stool by Christmas – and the original Sabbath line-up, with keyboardist Geoff Nichols, went on to play special gigs, tours and Ozzfest headlines with one disruption, in 1998, when Ward took some time out after a heart attack.

Reunion, a live album recorded at the second of two nights at Birmingham NEC in England on December 5, 1997, was released the following October, reaching number 41 in the UK and number 11 in the US. It included two new Sabbath studio tracks, "Psycho Man" and "Selling My Soul". The band then starting rehearsing, with the express intention of writing more material for an album.

Ozzy reported that although the chemistry onstage was immediate and exhilarating, the studio sessions were different, because all four members had become used to their own ways of doing things.

He considered: "It was kinda like meeting up with your first girlfriend years after and giving her a quickie for old times' sake. It sort of worked but yet it didn't. We couldn't recreate the same attitude. Back in the day we were all fucked up, and that was something that we weren't gonna do this time around."

Asked about his relationship with Ozzy, Tony Iommi has said: "When we talk, we get on fine. We did have our disagreements from years ago, but as time goes by, you think, 'Well, what's it all about?'"

"It was great to get back together. We were all in the right frame of mind to appreciate what we got. It's taken the years to sit back and look at it and go, 'Bloody hell!' We're lucky we're able to get back together and go out and play." He added: "We've got a unique sound that none of us have been able to recreate with any other players."

Bill Ward, admitting that it took him a long time to readjust to the band, said: "The end result was that I felt fantastic about the touring. I feel fantastic about the other guys as well."

Friends reunited

He added: "One of the beautiful things about Black Sabbath is that when we are backstage or in the studio or in rehearsals, we will have a cup of tea at about four in the afternoon, and we all sit down and we talk about what is wrong with us. We will talk about needing a new pair of glasses or we will ask, 'How's your stomach?' or 'How's your shoulder?'"

Geezer Butler, who repaired his friendship with Ozzy to help in his solo career, simply said: "Without a doubt, Ozzy is the craziest person I've ever met. Son Of Sam is a close second. I've seen him take a crap on some guy's car. For no reason. He's crazy. That was two days after I'd met him. And he's not mellowed with age. He's just more subtle now…"

Ozzy said of the reformations: "We gave each other space and respect, and it worked. All the juvenile shit-slinging, slagging and petty jealousies have finally gone. We're too fucking old, and I think we all realize the strengths we have together when we're on that stage…

"It's a weird deal. There's something magical between Tony Iommi, Geezer Butler and myself that is beyond explaining. It's this invisible fucking magic that just happens when we're up there." And, as all the best tabloid writers say, he refused to rule out further reunions.

"I can't say whether it's the final, *final* show ever unless one of us dies. I shouldn't say that. Last time I said, 'Well, at least we're all still alive,' Bill Ward dropped to the floor with a heart attack. He's doing fine now – though we do have to kickstart him before we do a show."

Kickstarting his own career, Ozzy formed a band comprising bassist Robert Trujillo (ex-Suicidal

Tendencies), drummer Mike Bordin and the returning Zakk Wylde. With producer Tim Palmer also adding guitars and keyboards and Ozzy again bringing in outside songwriters, they recorded *Down To Earth*.

According to Ozzy, it was partly named after Sabbath's early incarnation as Earth. "It's all down to Earth that I came here," he elaborated. And also, "I like to think I'm a down-to-earth sort of guy."

Having spent so much time in Sabbath mode, Ozzy approached the album with trepidation.

"I thought, 'Where the fuck do I fit into today's world?' I mean, I can't do this rap shit, or these big, Satan, growling voices."

In the event, he picked up pretty much from where he left off, with a mixture of vintage Ozz-rock and ballads. The emphasis is strongly on the hard stuff, although the production strides into modern territory and away from the filthy, Neanderthal grind of yesteryear. This horrified the hard-line fans who for some time had been accusing Ozzy of selling out because of his increasingly commercial objectives.

The album was released in October 2001 in the aftermath of the world-shattering events of September 11 – events which would colour Ozzy's own view of his work and responsibilities.

Together again: Iommi, Ozzy and Butler

"What, me? Rejoin Sabbath?"

Gets me Through

"I'm not the kind of person you think I am/I'm not the Antichrist or the Iron Man…"

Ozzy was directly addressing his fans, setting the record straight for any remaining, deluded souls who might have been under the wrong impression. (They're still out there, scattered across America.)

"I'm just a guy trying to give people a good night out," insisted Ozzy. "I'm like a conductor of madness, but a fun madness, not a violent madness."

One devotee recently felt obliged to point out the long-time espousal of pacifism by Ozzy and his co-writers. In a website posting, the writer enlightens readers: "If you actually pay attention to the lyrics, you'll see a lot of the songs are about telling people to stop fighting one another and love each other or instead we will eventually destroy ourselves. 'War Pigs', 'Children Of The Grave' and 'Thank God For The Bomb' are just a few examples of this."

"Some people think I've got supernatural powers," sighed Ozzy. "I'm not the Antichrist, I'm not the Iron Man. I'm just me. I bleed, I hurt, I smile, I laugh, I cry, I get worried like anybody else does. In fact, I do a lot of worrying, especially in today's climate since the fucking

Twin Towers got blasted and the Pentagon. I was in New York when that went down."

Subsequent to the atrocities, Ozzy toned down scenes of explosions in the video for "Gets Me Through", the album's first single, and changed the name of his forthcoming tour with Rob Zombie from Black Christmas to A Night Of Merry Mayhem.

The main thrust of "Gets Me Through" is an emotional thank you to fans for their continuing support, which, Ozzy says, saw him through his darkest hours. And he hopes that their loyalty will "never stop".

All this is transmitted in a riffing fury, following in the grand tradition of thumping Osbourne album openers.

Dreamer

He'd always loved Lennon and McCartney, and "Dreamer" is John, pure and simple, at the piano. "People say it's like Ozzy's 'Imagine'," said Ozzy. "And I take that as a compliment."

Like "Mother Earth" from the *Blizzard Of Ozz* album, "Dreamer" not only takes its musical inspiration from the Beatle but also frets about man's abuse of the natural world.

"You may say I'm a dreamer," sang Lennon.

"I'm just a dreamer," repeats Ozzy, years later.

"I hope some day you'll join us/And the world will live as one." ventured Lennon.

"It would be nice if we could live as one," echoes Ozzy, roving from the plight of the planet to an idealistic vision of humanity.

Ozzy commented: "I've always been concerned [about environmental issues]. Going back to Sabbath, I talked about that in several songs. It's always been in my mind, not so much for me, but I'd like somewhat of a life for my kids and their kids…

"I didn't go, 'Oh, fuck it, they just blew New York up, I better write a song about it.' [He wouldn't have had time anyway, given the timing of the album's release.] It's just one of those songs that's hopeful…

"It could be inspirational for a lot of people. I hope people in the world who are suffering can get some satisfaction and comfort from any one of my songs. There's a lot of sad people around the world right now."

He confirmed: "That's another song that came from nowhere. That was written a long, long time ago… It's not that I tried to copy "Imagine", but it's in that kind of a vein. It lends itself to a bit of hope. It's very positive."

"Dreamer" inadvertently became a plea for a harmonious future following the terrible grief and panic, conflict and fear arising from September 11.

"Don't worry kids…"

"I don't drink, I don't get stoned, and now my trainer says I've gotta stop drinking sodas."

Ozzy told MTV: "I think that the whole Western hemisphere [sic] kind of got to have a rethink about what they're gonna do. Suddenly, about two weeks later, I thought to myself, 'What was going on before the 11th of September?'"

What was going on *after* September 11 was Ozzy's performance at a World Trade Center benefit at Meadowlands, New Jersey, on December 23, donating the proceeds to a charity run by controversial radio presenter Howard Stern. He said of his financial gesture: "I trust Howard, and we know that the money is gonna go to where it's supposed to go to."

After the show, Ozzy was presented with an iron cross made from steel from the ruined towers by a New York City fireman and policeman.

Released as a single to capitalize on the success of "The Osbournes", "Dreamer" scored a massive number 4 hit in the US, charting in the lower teens in the UK.

Junkie

"A gut-wrenching fever, addicted to death/You don't give a fuck if it means your last breath…"

Another song about drug addiction and, specifically, the "beautiful flower" – heroin – "Junkie" looks at denial, craving and self-destruction. Its graphic descriptions act as a warning – from someone who knows a thing or two about narcotics.

By now, Ozzy had successfully given up all his favourite drugs, and he wasn't drinking either (although there were, and still are, rumours of the occasional tumble off the wagon). He had even quit tobacco, which interestingly he called "the worst addiction of my life", after 40 years of Old Holborn roll-ups and Cuban cigars.

The man reputed to have once snorted a line of ants for a laugh is not self-righteous in "Junkie" or in real life: he readily admits that things can get pretty boring around sobriety.

"... I will never wear a silly hat onstage!"

He said: "I don't drink, I don't get stoned, and now my trainer says I've gotta stop drinking sodas. I might as well shoot myself in the face. There's fuck all left, you know?"

He also revealed: "My biggest addiction these days is exercise. I run every day. I'll probably be next to Jimmy Savile [the veteran British TV presenter-turned-runner] next year running the fucking marathon. I only take pills now for clinical reasons, not to get stoned any more. All the stuff I did left me with some neurological problems – I'm a manic depressive, a nutter. Sharon says she'll second that."

Musically, "Junkie" is a highly charged rocker, although some critics have found it a little too formulaic, uneventful. It was composed by Ozzy with Aerosmith songwriter Marti Frederiksen, bassist Robert Trujillo and Joe Holmes, the guitarist who accompanied Ozzy on the Retirement Sucks tour.

Zakk Wylde, who plays on *Down To Earth*, unusually receives no writing credits on the album. He recalled being approached by Ozzy. "He said, 'Zakk, I don't want to have to go through the whole writing process. I've got all these songs I want to do, can you come in and just play your ass off?' So I went down there, drank some fucking beer, and played. We had a blast making the record. And then Sharon said, 'If you can, just write a couple of extra tracks for the record.'

"So I'd be down in rehearsal, pumping riffs and songs out every fucking day. And Ozz was like, 'That song is like beyond-stupid heavy, I don't want to use that one.' It came down to the point where Ozzy said, 'Well, I want to use the songs I got, and that's that.' I was like, 'No problem, man.' It's fucking his record at the end of the day. 'Whatever you want to fucking do, I'm here for you.'"

Alive

The backbone of the album is solid, accomplished but unsurprising heavy rock music, and "Alive" is a typical example: slow, moody verses build up to full-on power surges, with lead and background vocals adding to the dramatic effect.

Wylde's guitar locks on to the hard rhythm section, with Trujillo and Mike Bordin respecting and robustly fulfilling their roles, but not overstepping the mark.

Bordin, who grew up "worshipping" Ozzy and Sabbath, was thrilled to be playing with his hero. He said: "For me, sitting at the back, it's important to be mindful of what's happening out front. It's about the love, and trying to do it right. You know like when you play [American] football and there's a guy who holds the ball and then there's the guy that kicks it? Well, I'm kind of holding the ball for Ozzy. I have to try and make sure he can do his job. It's important to remember that it's a supporting gig. You're the foundation, the skeleton, and not the pretty exterior. But that's a lot of fun too."

Along with tracks such as "Facing Hell", "Running Out Of Time" and "Can You Hear Them?", "Alive" is filled with revelations of inner tumult, chaotic flashes from a life lived well – or not so well – and fears about the onset of old age and death: the stuff of a mid-life crisis.

"I don't have any plans to go anywhere/You know I'm alive."

That, in itself, is a miracle of sorts. Ozzy said, "One time I bought a pound of grass and took four tablets of mescalin, a quarter of an ounce of cocaine and a bottle of tequila, and I was out of my tree for a week. I had the worst fucking time of my entire life. I thought, 'That's it, I've done it now. I'm going to be here forever.'"

And he acknowledged: "I know I should be dead. I didn't burn the candle at both ends – I burnt it every fucking which way the fucking thing can be held."

Other tracks on the album are the polished, tunefully metallic "No Easy Way Out"; the tearful but hot-rocking "That I Never Had"; "You Know... (Part 1)", a father's short but sensitive apology to a child, believed to be Jessica, Ozzy's daughter by his first marriage; and "Black Illusion", which depicts an oppressive scenario, conveyed musically and lyrically.

Tracks on the preceding Black Sabbath album, *Reunion*, are: "War Pigs", "Beyond The Wall Of Sleep", "N.I.B.", "Fairies Wear Boots", "Electric Funeral", "Sweet Leaf", "Spiral Architect", "Into The Void", "Snowblind", "Sabbath Bloody Sabbath", "Iron Man", "Children Of The Grave", "Paranoid", "Psycho Man" and "Selling My Soul".

Tracks on the earlier Ozzy compilation album *The Ozzman Cometh* are: "Black Sabbath", "War Pigs", "Goodbye To Romance (Live)", "Crazy Train (Live)", "Mr Crowley (Live)", "Over The Mountain (Live)", "Paranoid (Live)", "Bark At The Moon", "Shot In The Dark", "Crazy Babies", "No More Tears", "Mama, I'm Coming Home (Live)", "I Just Want You", "I Don't Want To Change the World" and (on the CD) "Fairies Wear Boots" and "Beyond The Wall Of Sleep".

And so to the Present

In 2002 – some 33 years after the formation of Black Sabbath – Ozzy Osbourne became famous beyond his wildest dreams.

It was the sort of fame that touched people who had never heard of Sabbath or Blizzard Of Ozz, that reached into living rooms around the world and mesmerized the occupants.

This was, of course, the result of 'The Osbournes', a brilliant masterstroke by Sharon Osbourne, who saw in the idea of a reality TV show the chance of a fabulous financial security for her family.

Cameras followed the Osbournes day and night as they moved into a new Hollywood mansion, upset the neighbours and each other, and ran a gamut of human behaviour and emotion that, for all of the wealthy and glamorous setting, struck a chord with the humblest of viewers.

Airing in America in March and in Europe a couple of months later, "The Osbournes" racked up record-breaking audience figures for a new programme on MTV, with ratings racing to the highest-ever in the station's history.

Ozzy, stumbling from one room to another, lurching from one domestic crisis to the next, is unwittingly heroic as he negotiates life's obstacles with a barrage of swearing, a supreme mastery of the blunt one-liner, a perfect sense of comic timing and an unwavering sense of duty to his wife and children, with whom he interacts unconventionally but devotedly.

The series has also made superstars of the feisty Sharon and battling teenagers Jack and Kelly. Jack, a podgy and eccentric individual, has recently been photographed with the gorgeous model and would-be actress Catalina who declares that she adores his company and not, of course, the celebrity of his family. And Kelly's hormonal and rebellious outbursts are typical of scenes experienced in many a regular household as she bickers with her brother, fights with her mother and worries her father to distraction.

(The elder daughter, Aimee, opted out of the scrutiny

Home, sweet home

Kelly and Jack: a rare moment of togetherness

The Walk Of Fame

"Nothing freaks me out any more."

While friends have applauded Ozzy's courage in submitting to such an experiment, with Bill Ward saying that "I am going to wave a big fucking banner and say, 'Hurray, Hurray!'", Ozzy is characteristically bewildered by the hoopla, and doesn't trust it.

Proud to be a "real, true, working-class hero," he nevertheless told Rolling Stone magazine: "I'm the flavour of the month. I know I'm this year's version of Roseanne Barr. I know the bubble will burst, and I'm going to be yesterday's news. But I'm not letting any of this get in the way of my music. I can still rock like a son of a bitch."

With a second series of "The Osbournes" filmed, Ozzy is still more interested in his musical legacy, in the influence that Black Sabbath brought to bear on generations of rock musicians and in a solo career that saw him sell millions of albums.

"I was on the road in the mid-Eighties with Metallica opening the shows and I heard them playing Sabbath songs in their dressing room before they went on," he said. "I thought they were taking the piss. It wasn't until much later that I found out how much of an influence Black Sabbath were on them."

Modestly, he insisted: "I don't really feel like the father of metal or rock, more like a big brother. . ."

Somehow, Ozzy remains resolutely grounded.

With a second Grammy under his belt for Black Sabbath's "Iron Man" from the *Reunion* album, with a Sabbath star on Sunset Boulevard, and with one of his own presented on April 12, 2002, he remarked:

"Everybody in the record industry wants to get a platinum disc. I've got plenty of them. I've got Grammys. This year, I got a star on the Hollywood Walk of Fame. Nothing freaks me out any more."

Marilyn Manson, present at the Walk of Fame ceremony, seems more impressed. He said: "This star proves that it is quite obvious that Ozzy has managed to succeed while remaining insane and strangely happy despite his various crimes against man and nature."

Ozzy has been celebrated not only by the rock community but by a whole range of performers: he has collaborated with such diverse talents as Lemmy and Kim Basinger, Lita Ford and Miss Piggy, the "South Park" ensemble and the Wu-Tang Clan, rapper Busta Rhymes and "gothadelic industrimetal Brooklyn dirtbags" Type O Negative.

Ozzy has been sought after for film appearances and honoured by tribute albums.

And his company has been requested by the highest in the land. On May 4, he attended a dinner hosted by President Bush at the White House – the building that the FBI once accused him of plotting to piss over.

He told Rolling Stone of that occasion: "I felt like the in-house joke. I was really nervous. But it was like Beatlemania. The press were going nuts. Everything that has happened to me in the last six months has been incredible. Two years ago, I'm thinking, 'I'm 52. I'll peter off doing Ozzfest once a year and bow out gracefully.' All of a sudden, someone throws a success grenade in the room."

Sharon: fighting her biggest battle

backstage was great. I was there with Sir Paul McCartney, Bryan Adams, Joe Cocker, all in the dressing tent. It was like sitting in a bar with every celebrity in the world."

Ozzy succeeded in restraining his language, although Sharon did let slip the F-word in front of Prince Charles' escort, Camilla Parker-Bowles.

And Ozzy's over-riding impression of the Queen of England? "She's got the greatest skin for a woman of her age."

The success of "The Osbournes" effectively restricted any other plans Ozzy may have been making for the immediate future. Fans were therefore treated in June 2002 to yet another live album, *Live At Budokan*, which was recorded four months earlier and features his *Down To Earth* line-up of Wylde, Trujillo and Bordin, plus keyboardist John Sinclair.

It should have been a wonderful year for Ozzy, but fate threw tragedy his way at the same time.

On March 26, drummer Randy Castillo - Ozzy and Motley Crue veteran – died at 51 from cancer.

Then, devastatingly for Ozzy – so "hysterical" he had to be sedated – his wife Sharon was diagnosed with colon cancer in July and underwent immediate surgery. Within days it was revealed from lymph-node tests that the disease had spread.

"Why did they have to find it in my bum, of all places?" demanded a typically ballsy Sharon, who then agreed to have her chemotherapy treatment filmed for an "interesting" element in the next series of "The Osbournes".

As someone who has met and appreciated Sharon Osbourne, this author hopes and trusts that she will make a full recovery.

And as for Ozzy – his place in the history books is assured, for all the right reasons.

Way back in time, he said: "I'll never be mellow. I'd sooner die than become a boring old fart. I'm still as much of a loon as I ever was. I like being a little crazy. It makes people respect you. They never take you for granted, that's for sure."

They still don't.

And the world's favourite, well-meaning and muddled dad can undoubtedly lay to rest the fear he expressed only months before "The Osbournes" stormed the world: 'I don't relish my tombstone. It'll be: "Ozzy Osbourne, the man who bit the head off a bat."'

Tracks on *Live At Budokan* are: "I Don't Know", "That I Never Had", "Believer", "Junkie", "Mr Crowley", "Gets Me Through", "No More Tears", "I Don't Want To Change The World", "Road To Nowhere", "Crazy Train", "Mama, I'm Coming Home", "Bark At The Moon" and "Paranoid".

Only a month later, the former Prince of Darkness entertained HM The Queen at her Golden Jubilee concert at Buckingham Palace with a rendition of "Paranoid".

Commented Ozzy, again to Rolling Stone: "Prince William said to me later, 'It would have been great if you had done 'Black Sabbath'. If I had done 'Black Sabbath', the fucking royal box would have turned to stone and the Archbishop of Canterbury would have had to douse them in holy water.

"... But everyone, the royal family, all the princes, was headbanging, giving it plenty. And the atmosphere

CHRONOLOGY

February 19 1948
Tony Iommi born
May 5 1948
Bill Ward born
December 3 1948
John Michael Osbourne (Ozzy) born
July 17 1949
Geezer Butler born
1962
Ozzy makes his singing debut with The Black Panthers
1965
Ozzy serves two months in HMP Winson Green for burglary, larceny, assault and possession of dope
1966–69
Ozzy drops in and out of bands such as Music Machine, Approach, Rare Breed (with Geezer Butler) and The Polka Tulk Blues Band, later Polka Tulk and Earth, with Iommi, Butler and Ward
1969
Earth change their name to Black Sabbath
February 13 1970
Black Sabbath's self-titled, debut album released on Vertigo in the UK
January 1970 and March 1970
Black Sabbath's debut single, "Evil Woman, Don't Play Your Games With Me" released by Fontana and then Vertigo
June 1970
Black Sabbath album released on Warners in America
August 1970
"Paranoid" single released to huge success
1970
Band smoking huge amounts of hashish and drinking heavily
September 1970
Paranoid album establishes classic sound of Black Sabbath
1971
Sabbath liberally indulge in cocaine, acid and pills in America, promoting *Paranoid* and *Master Of Reality* albums
1971
Ozzy marries Birmingham girlfriend Thelma Mayfair
1970–71

September 1972
Sabbath's fourth album released under the name *Vol. 4* after the record company vetoes "Snowblind" because of its cocaine reference
1972
Ozzy's daughter Jessica born
1972
Band friendships splintering, with an unhappy Bill Ward sent home from the studio
1973
Black Sabbath find inspiration for *Sabbath Bloody Sabbath* in a haunted castle
Winter 1973
Ozzy first thinks about leaving Sabbath
1974–75
Managerial disputes lead to prolonged legal action and 1975's *Sabotage* track, "The Writ"
1975
Ozzy's son Louis born
Autumn 1977
Amid the band's worsening relationships and drugs and booze marathons, Ozzy leaves Black Sabbath for three months, to be replaced by Dave Ward. During this period, Ozzy's father dies. His marriage is now

January 1978
Ozzy rejoins Black Sabbath to record *Never Say Die*
1979
Ozzy sacked from Sabbath by Bill Ward. Spends three months in shock in an LA hotel room
1979
Ozzy forms Blizzard Of Ozz, introducing young guitar hero Randy Rhoads
September 1980
Blizzard Of Ozz album released. Includes controversial track "Suicide Solution". Ozzy is later sued by three sets of parents alleging that the song was responsible for their children's suicides
Autumn 1980
Blizzard Of Ozz perform for the first time, in Scotland
1981
Ozzy divorced from Thelma
Winter 1981
Ozzy bites the head of a live dove at a record company conference
January 20 1982
Ozzy bites the head off a bat onstage in Des Moines, Iowa
February 1982
Ozzy pisses on the Alamo in Texas
March 19 1982
Randy Rhoads killed in plane crash
July 4 1982
Ozzy marries Sharon Arden
November 1982
Talk Of The Devil releases Ozzy from his obligations to Jet Records. He also leaves manager Don Arden, Sharon's dad, leading to a long and bitter estrangement of father and daughter
September 2 1983
Aimee Osbourne born
December 1983
Guitarist Jake E Lee makes his Ozzy debut on *Bark At The Moon*
New Year's Eve 1983
James Jollimore murders three people after listening to *Bark At The Moon*
October 27 1984
Kelly Osbourne born
July 13 1985
Black Sabbath reunite for Live Aid concert
November 8 1985
Jack Osbourne born
1987
Ozzy recruits Zakk Wylde, his longest-serving guitarist
1988
Ozzy openly admits his alcoholism, having sought help over several years from AA and Betty Ford

Winter 1988
Geezer Butler joins the band touring *No Rest For The Wicked*
August 1989
Ozzy plays the Moscow Music Peace Festival
September 2 1989
Ozzy charged with attempted murder after trying to kill Sharon in a drunken rage. Charges are dropped on condition Ozzy goes into rehab
1991
Ozzy conquers drugs and booze addictions
November 1992
Ozzy 'retires' after final gig in California, culminating in a Sabbath reunion
1993
Ozzy bored with retirement
1994
Ozzy returns to the studio to record *Ozzmosis*
1995
Ozzy recruits live guitarist Joe Holmes, a Randy Rhoads pupil
September 1996
The first Ozzfest, a two-day event in America
1997
Ozzy, Tony Iommi and Geezer Butler reunite as Black Sabbath with drummer Mike Bordin for Ozzfest
Christmas 1997
Bill Ward rejoins the original Sabbath for gigs and tours
1988
Bill Ward suffers heart attack, but later rejoins Sabbath
April 10 2001
Ozzy's mother dies
October 2001
Ozzy resumes solo career with *Down To Earth*
December 23 2001
Ozzy plays World Trade Center benefit in New Jersey
March 2002
"The Osbournes" opens on MTV America to immediate success
March 26 2002
Long-time Ozzy drummer Randy Castillo dies from cancer
April 12 2002
Ozzy receives a star on Hollywood's Walk Of Fame
May 4 2002
Ozzy has dinner with President Bush
June 3 2002
Ozzy sings for Queen Elizabeth II in her garden at Buckingham Palace
July 2002
Sharon Osbourne has surgery for colon cancer, later discovering it has spread. She begins a course of chemotherapy

Discography

These are Ozzy's official releases. They do not include reissues or compilations, except where these were career releases.

Black Sabbath with Ozzy

SINGLES

Jan 70 Evil Woman (Don't Play Your Games With Me)/Wicked World (UK Fontana)

Mar 70 Evil Woman (Don't Play Your Games With Me)/Wicked World (UK Vertigo)

Aug 70 Paranoid/The Wizard (UK Vertigo/ US Warners, Nov 70)

Jan 72 Iron Man/Electric Funeral (US Warners)

Sep 72 Tomorrow's Dream/Laguna Sunrise (UK Vertigo/US Warners)

Oct 73 Sabbath Bloody Sabbath/Changes (UK WWA/US Warners)

Feb 76 Am I Going Insane (Radio)/Hole In The Sky (UK NEMS/US Warners)

Nov 76 It's Alright/Rock'n'Roll Doctor (US Warners)

May 78 Never Say Die!/She's Gone (UK Vertigo)

Sep 78 Hard Road/Symptom Of The Universe (UK Vertigo)

Dec 99 Black Mass EP (UK NMC)

ALBUMS

Feb 70 Black Sabbath (UK Vertigo/US Warners, Jul 70)

Sep 70 Paranoid (UK Vertigo/US Warners, Feb 71)

Aug 71 Master Of Reality (UK Vertigo/US Warners)

Sep 72 Black Sabbath Vol 4 (UK Vertigo /US Warners, Oct 72)

Dec 73 Sabbath Bloody Sabbath (UK WWA/US

Warners, Jan 74)

Sep 75 Sabotage (UK NEMS/US Warners)

Feb 76 We Sold Our Soul For Rock'n'Roll (compilation) (UK NEMS/US Warners)

Oct 76 Technical Ecstacy (UK Vertigo/US Warners)

Oct 78 Never Say Die! (UK Vertigo/US Warners)

Oct 98 Reunion (Epic)

OZZY OSBOURNE'S BLIZZARD OF OZZ
SINGLES

Sep 80 Crazy Train/You Looking At Me Looking At You (UK Jet)

Nov 80 Mr Crowley (Live)/You Said It All (Live) (UK Jet/US Jet-CBS, Apr 82)

Apr 81 Crazy Train/Steal Away (The Night) (UK Jet)

ALBUMS

Sep 80 Ozzy Osbourne's Blizzard Of Ozz (UK Jet/US Jet-CBS, Mar 81)

OZZY OSBOURNE
SINGLES

Nov 81 Over The Mountain/I Don't Know (US Jet-CBS)

Nov 81 Little Dolls/Tonight (US Jet-CBS)

Dec 82 Symptom Of The Universe (Live)/NIB (Live) (US Jet-CBS)

Feb 83 Iron Man (Live)/Paranoid (Live) (US Jet-CBS)

Nov 83 Bark At The Moon/One Up On The B-Side (UK Epic/US CBS Assoc)

Dec 83 Bark At The Moon/Spiders (US CBS Assoc)

Mar 84 So Tired/Forever (Live) (UK Epic/US CBS Assoc)

Mar 84 So Tired/Bark At The Moon (Live) (UK Epic/US CBS Assoc)

Jan 86 Shot In The Dark/Rock'n'Roll Rebel (UK Epic)

Jul 86 The Ultimate Sin/Lightning Strikes (UK Epic)

Oct 88 Miracle Man/Crazy Babies (UK Epic)

Oct 88 Miracle Man/Man You Said It All (US CBS Assoc)

Feb 89 Crazy Babies/The Demon Alcohol (US CBS Assoc)

Sep 91 No More Tears/SIN (UK Epic/US Epic Assoc)

Nov 91 Mama I'm Coming Home/Don't Blame Me (UK Epic/US Epic Assoc, Feb 92)

Jun 93 Changes (Live)/Changes/No More Tears/Desire (UK Epic/US Epic Assoc)

Nov 95 Perry Mason/Living With The Enemy (UK Epic/US Epic Assoc)

Aug 96 I Just Want You/Aimee/Voodoo Dancer (UK Epic/US Epic Assoc)

Feb 02 Dreamer/Gets Me Through (UK Epic/US Epic Assoc)

ALBUMS

Oct 81 Diary Of A Madman (UK Jet/US Jet-CBS)

Nov 82 Talk Of The Devil (UK Jet/US Jet-CBS, titled Speak Of The Devil)

Dec 83 Bark At The Moon (UK Epic/US CBS Assoc)

Feb 86 The Ultimate Sin (UK Epic/US CBS Assoc)

May 87 Tribute (Live) (UK Epic/US Epic Assoc)

Oct 88 No Rest For The Wicked (UK Epic/US CBS Assoc)

Feb 90 Just Say Ozzy (Live) (UK Epic/US CBS Assoc)

Dec 91 No More Tears (UK Epic/US Epic Assoc)

Jun 93 Live & Loud (Live) (UK Epic/US Epic Assoc)

Oct 95 Ozzmosis (UK Epic/US Epic Assoc)

Nov 97 The Ozzman Cometh – The Best Of (UK Epic/US Epic Assoc)

Oct 01 Down To Earth (UK Epic/US Epic Assoc)

Jun 02 Live At Budokan (UK Epic/US Epic Assoc)

Index

A

AC/DC 8, 75
"After Forever" 20, 35
"Air Dance" 68
Airey, Don 73, 92
Alamo 6, 83
Aldridge, Tommy 81, 101
"Alive" 135-6
Altman, Billy 55
"Am I Going Insane" 59
Anderson, Thomas 97
Approach 12
Arden, Don 54, 72, 94
Arden, Sharon 72, 81, 88-9, 93, 94, 112-13, 127-8, 131, 137, 139
Aycock, Andrew 92

B

Baksh, Dave 120
Bangs, Lester 35
Bark at the Moon 90-9
"Bark At The Moon" 95, 97
Beinhorn, Michael 122, 125
"Believer" 89
Bian, Roger 16, 26
Birmingham (England) 10
Black Panthers, The 12
Black Sabbath: *Black Sabbath* 14-21; Christian message 35; *Master of Reality* 30-7; *Never Say Die!* 60-9; origins10-13; Ozzy Osbourne 12-13, 62, 65, 121, 131-2; *Paranoid* 22-8; *Sabbath Bloody Sabbath* 46-50; *Sabotage* 54-9; satanism 7, 16-17; 32-3, 34; *Technical Ecstasy* 62; *Vol 4* 38-43, 46
Black Sabbath 14-21
"Black Sabbath" 17
Blizzard of Ozz 70-9
"Bloodbath In Paradise" 106, 108
"Blow On A Jug" 59
Bonham, John 26, 28
Bordin, Mike 132, 135-6
"Breakout" 68-9
Buckingham Palace 139
Bush, George W. 138
Butler, Geezer 10, 12, 13, 16, 17, 18, 20, 23, 28, 32-3, 34, 35, 36, 40, 43, 48, 49, 50, 57, 64, 65, 112, 124, 132

C

Carlson, Dylan 12
Castillo, Randy 139
Castronovo, Dean 122
"Centre Of Eternity" 98
"Chain, The" 69
"Changes" 40-1
"Children Of The Grave" 36
Clark, Steve 118
Cobain, Kurt 12, 44
Corgan, Billy 30
Costa, Don 94
"Cornucopia" 42-3
"Crazy Babies" 108
"Crazy Train" 74-5
Crow 20
Crowley, Aleister 79
Curry, Adam 112

D

Daisley, Bob 72, 74-5, 81, 86, 88, 89, 92, 93, 94, 98, 101, 103, 113, 118, 122
Def Leppard 118
"Demon Alcohol" 108-9
"Devil's Daughter" 105-6
Diary of a Madman 80-9
"Diary Of A Madman" 89
Dio, Ronnie James 72
"Dirty Women" 62
Down to Earth 130-6
"Dreamer" 133-4
Dubrow, Kevin 92
Dudas, Steve 127
Duncan, Jake 92
Durst, Fred 22

E

Earth 12-13
Elizabeth II 139
"Embryo" 36
"Evil Woman (Don't Play Your Games With Me) 20-1

F

"Fairies Wear Boots" 28
"Fluff" 50
"Flying High Again" 85-6, 88
Fredrickson, Marti 135
"FX" 43

G

"Get Me Through" 133
Gillis, Brad 94
"Goodbye To Romance" 75
Graff, Gary 116
Grohl, Dave 44
Guns N' Roses 123, 130

H

"Hand Of Doom" 28-9
"Hard Road, A" 69
headbanging 24
Henry's 12
Hetfield, James 52
"Hole In The Sky" 57-8
Holmes, Joe 124, 135
Hudson, Mark 127

I

"I Just Want You" 127
Inez, Mike 113, 18, 124
"Into The Void" 36
Iommi, Tony 10, 12, 13, 16, 17, 18, 23, 26, 28-9, 33-4, 40, 41, 46-7, 48, 57, 58-9, 62, 64-5, 68, 72
"Iron Man" 27-8

J

Jethro Tull 13
"Johnny Blade" 69
Jollimore, James 97
Jone, Allan 83
Jordison, Joey 80, 83
"Junior's Eyes" 68
"Junkie" 134-5
Just Say Ozzy 112

K

Kerrang! 26
Kerslake, Lee 73, 81, 85, 93
"Killing Yourself To Live" 50
King, Kerry 100

L

"Laguna Sunrise" 43, 59
LaVey, Anton 32
Led Zeppelin 12, 13, 23, 26
Lee, Alvin 13, 43
Lee, Jake E 94, 98-9, 101, 103
Lemmy 113, 116, 127
Lennon, John 133-4
Limp Bizkit 22
"Little Dolls" 89
Live and Loud 122
Live at Budokan 139
"Looking For Today" 50
"Lord Of This World" 36

M

Malone, Will 58
"Mama, I'm Coming Home" 116
Manson, Charles 32, 106, 108
Manson, Marilyn 14, 15, 138
Marriott, Steve 8, 127
Master of Reality 30-7
Meehan, Patrick 39, 54
"Megalomania" 58
Melody Maker 48
Metallica 52, 138
"Miracle Man" 105
"Mr Jesus" 59
"Mr Tinkertrain" 114

Mudvayne 70
Mushok, Mike 110
Music Machine 12
"My Little Man" 128
Mythology 10

N

"National Acrobat, A" 49
Nirvana 44
Never Say Die! 60-9
"Never Say Die!" 65, 68
Nevison, Ron 102
"NIB" 18, 20
No More Tears 110-19
"No More Tears" 116, 118
No Rest for the Wicked 100-9, 112
"Now You See It (Now You Don't)" 97-8
Nugent, Ted 90

O

"Old LA Tonight" 128-9
"Orchid" 36
Osbourne, Aimee 113, 137
Osbourne, Jack (father) 10, 16, 21, 62, 68, 128
Osbourne, Jack (son) 137
Osbourne, Kelly 137
Osbourne, Lillian 10
Osbourne, Ozzy: *Bark at the Moon* 90-9; Black Sabbath 12-13, 62, 65, 121, 131-2; *Blizzard of Ozz* 70-9; Buckingham Palace 139; *Diary of a Madman* 80-9; *Down to Earth* 130-6; drinking 77, 108-9, 118-19; early life 10, 12; groupies 39, 97; *Master of Reality* 31-2; *Never Say Die!* 64; *No More Tears* 110-19; *No Rest for the Wicked* 100-9; Ozzfest 124-5; *Ozzmosis 120-9; Paranoid* 23-4; and Randy Rhoads 8, 72-3; *Sabotage* 545, 576; *Sabbath Bloody Sabbath* 4, 557; on satanism 7, 16-17; 32-3, 34, 79; and Sharon Arden 72, 88-9, 112-13, 127-8; *Technical Ecstasy* 62; *The Ultimate Sin* 101-3; and Thelma Osbourne 88-9; and Tommy Ionni 40; *Vol 4* 39-40' "Who Are You?" 50

Osbourne, Thelma 88-9
Osbournes, The (documentary) 6, 137-8
"Over The Mountain" 85
"Over To You" 69
Ozzfest 124-5, 131
Ozzman Cometh, The 131
Ozzmosis 120-9

P

Palmer, Tim 132
Paradise, Matt C 35
Paranoid 22-8, 42
"Paranoid" 18, 26-7
"Perry Mason" 125, 127
Pine, Will 54
Plant, Robert 23
Polka Tulk 12
Polka Tulk Blues Band 12

R

Red Hot Chili Peppers 24-5
Rest, The 10
Reunion 131
Rhoads, Dolores 103
Rhoads, Randy 8, 72-3, 81, 85, 92-4, 103, 124
Roberts, Oral 105
Rolling Stone 35, 138, 139
Rollins, Henry 38
Rosen, Steve 24, 34, 40, 47, 50, 57, 64, 98, 128

S

Sabbath Bloody Sabbath 46-50, 55
"Sabbath Bloody Sabbath" 48
"Sabbra Cadabra" 50
Sabotage 54-9, 62
"St Vitus Dance" 43
Sanders, Alex 33
Sarzo, Rudy 81, 94
satanism 7, 16-17, 32-3, 34, 79
"Satanism and Heavy Metal: The Confusion Continues' (Paradise) 35
"SATO" 88-9
"See You On The Other Side" 127-8
"Shock Wave" 69
Scott, Bon 8, 75, 77
Simpson, Jim 12, 54
Slash 130
Slayer 100
Slipknot 80
Smashing Pumpkins, The 30
"Snowblind" 42
"So Tired" 98-9

"Solitude" 36
Soussan, Phil 101, 102-3
"Spiral Architect" 50
Stern, Howard 134
Stix, John 13, 48
"Suicide Solution" 75, 77, 97
Sum 41 120
"Supernaut" 41
"Supertzar" 58-9
Swaggart, Jimmy 105
"Sweet Leaf" 33-4
"Symptom Of The Universe" 57-8

T

Talk of the Devil 94
Technical Ecstasy 62
Ten Years After 13
"Thrill Of It All, The" 59
"Tomorrow's Dream" 40
Torme, Bernie 94
Tribbett, Greg 70
Tribute 103
Trujillo, Robert 132, 135

U

Ultimate Sin, The 101-3
"Under The Sun" 43

V

Vai, Steve 122, 128
Vallence, Jim 127
Van Halen 65
Vietnam 25
Vol 4 38-43, 46

W

Wakeman, Rick 47, 122
"War Pigs" 25-6, 42
Ward, Bill 10, 12, 21, 23, 24, 28, 34, 40-1, 42-3, 47, 48, 55, 64, 65, 69, 131-2, 138
Ward, Dave 62
Way, Pete 94
"Wheels Of Confusion" 40
White Zombie 60
"Who Are You?" 50
"Wizard, The" 18
Woodruffe, Gerald 55
Wright, Jeb 72, 86, 113
"Writ, The " 54, 59
Wylde, Zakk 8, 103, 106, 113, 114, 116, 118, 123, 128, 132, 135

Y

"You Can't Kill Rock'n'Roll" 88
Youngblood, Rachel 92

Z

Zombie, Rob 60
"Zombie Stomp" 118-19